Interactions Access
Reading/Writing

Interactions Access
Reading/Writing

4th Edition

Pamela Hartmann
Los Angeles Unified School District

James Mentel
Los Angeles Unified School District

McGraw-Hill Contemporary

McGraw-Hill/Contemporary

A Division of The **McGraw-Hill** Companies

Interactions Access Reading/Writing, 4th Edition

Published by McGraw-Hill/Contemporary, a business unit of The McGraw-Hill Companies, Inc., 1221 Avenue of the Americas, New York, NY 10020. Copyright © 2002, 1997, 1993 by The McGraw-Hill Companies, Inc. All rights reserved. No part of this publication may be reproduced or distributed in any form or by any means, or stored in a database or retrieval system, without the prior written consent of The McGraw-Hill Companies, Inc., including, but not limited to, in any network or other electronic storage or transmission, or broadcast for distance learning.

Some ancillaries, including electronic and print components, may not be available to customers outside the United States.

 This book is printed on recycled, acid-free paper containing 10% postconsumer waste.

3 4 5 6 7 8 9 0 QPD/QPD 0 9 8 7 6 5 4 3 2

ISBN 0–07–232974–2
ISBN 0–07–112394–6 (ISE)

Editorial director: *Tina B. Carver*
Series editor: *Annie Sullivan*
Developmental editor: *Louis Carrillo*
Director of marketing and sales: *Thomas P. Dare*
Project manager: *Sheila M Frank*
Production supervisor: *Laura Fuller*
Coordinators of freelance design: *Michelle M. Meerdink/David W. Hash*
Interior designer: *Michael Warrell, Design Solutions*
Photo research coordinator: *John C. Leland*
Photo research: *Amelia Ames Hill Associates/Amy Bethea*
Supplement coordinator: *Genevieve Kelley*
Compositor: *David Corona Design*
Typeface: *10.5/12 Times Roman*
Printer: *Quebecor World Dubuque, IA*

The credits section for this book begins on page 167 and is considered an extension of the copyright page.

INTERNATIONAL EDITION ISBN 0–07–112394–6
Copyright © 2002. Exclusive rights by The McGraw-Hill Companies, Inc., for manufacture and export. This book cannot be re-exported from the country to which it is sold by McGraw-Hill. The International Edition is not available in North America.

www.mhcontemporary.com/interactionsmosaic

Interactions Access
Reading/Writing

Interactions Access **Reading/Writing**

Boost your students' academic success!

Interactions Mosaic, 4ᵗʰ edition is the newly revised five-level, four-skill comprehensive ESL/EFL series designed to prepare students for academic content. The themes are integrated across proficiency levels and the levels are articulated across skill strands. The series combines communicative activities with skill-building exercises to boost students' academic success.

Interactions Mosaic, 4ᵗʰ edition features

■ updated content

■ five videos of authentic news broadcasts

■ expansion opportunities through the Website

■ new audio programs for the listening/speaking and reading books

■ an appealing fresh design

■ user-friendly instructor's manuals with placement tests and chapter quizzes

In This Chapter gives students a preview of the upcoming material.

Chapter **3**

Friends and Family

IN THIS CHAPTER

You will read about changes in families in different countries. You will also read about an American tradition—a family reunion—and you will write a letter about yourself.

PART 1   **Volunteers**

Before You Read

1   Look at the photos and answer the questions with a partner or a group.

1. Who are these people?
2. What are they doing? Why?

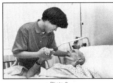

Photo 2

Photo 1

Photo 3

2   **Vocabulary Preview.**   Sometimes a colon (:) can help you unders...
If you know the key word or words on one side of the colon, then y...
the meaning of the word or words on the other side of the colon...

Examples

There are terrible diseases: AIDS, cancer, and TB.

What are some examples of diseases?   <u>AIDS, cancer, and T...</u>

She cooked some wonderful foods: stews, casseroles, and sou...

What are stews, casseroles, and soufflés?   <u>some wonderful foo...</u>

Preliminary activities provide scaffolding to help students deal with authentic language.

Photos and illustrations activate prior knowledge of the reading topic.

Vocabulary Preview allows students to anticipate unknown vocabulary.

Vocabulary and language-learning strategies for alphabetizing, following directions, and reading graphics give students comprehension and self-assessment.

Discussing the Reading encourages students to contribute their own opinions on high-interest subjects relating to the readings.

Now read the paragraph. Focus on the phrases, not the separate words:

> Men and women sometimes seem to speak different languages. They like to talk about different things. Sometimes they don't listen to each other. A woman makes a suggestion, but her husband doesn't understand. A man tries to help, but his wife doesn't like it. Maybe they should go to language school!

4   **Building Vocabulary.**   Complete the following sentences. Circle the letters of the answers. There is one answer for each blank.

1. Their _____ are very important to them.
   - a. leader
   - b. friends
   - c. cultural
   - d. friendship

2. Could you please give me some _____?
   - a. information
   - b. important
   - c. active
   - d. suggestion

3. Maybe we should _____.
   - a. advice
   - b. happen
   - c. show
   - d. apologize

4. That information is _____.
   - a. brag
   - b. wrong
   - c. orders
   - d. argue

Are the meanings of the following words similar or different? Write S (similar) or D (different) on the lines.

1. <u>S</u> sleepy—tired
2. ____ suggestions—activities
3. ____ family—relatives
4. ____ waste—deficit
5. ____ apologize—brag
6. ____ leader—position

Discussing the Reading

5   In small groups, talk about your answers to the following questions.

1. Are people in your country similar to or different from the man and woman pictured on page 75?
2. If you're a woman, what do you talk about with other women? What do you talk about with men? If you're a man, what do you talk about with other men? What do you talk about with women?

Real-life reading connects the classroom to real life through ads, forms, brochures, and other realia.

PART 3 **Tours and Using a Travel Map**

1 Look at the photos and read about the different tours that follow. Don't worry about new words. Then answer the questions that follow.

Adventure Tours, Inc.

Do you want something different? Something exciting?
Here is our new group of tours.

1. Tibet Tour
Six days in one of the most unusual counties in Asia. Very few tourists go to Tibet. All around are the tallest mountains in the world. You will visit beautiful monasteries and crowded street markets. You will also see wonderful Tibetan dancing.
Length of trip: 14 days. Group size: 16
Cost: $6,000

2. Maui Bicycling Tour
Ride a bicycle around the most beautiful tropical island in the world. You will swim in the clear, warm tropical water, and go camping in the beautiful national parks.
Length of trip: 7 days. Group size: 9–12
Cost: $695

3. Cooking Tour
Do you like French food? Do you like to cook? Visit Paris and seven other French cities. Visit the best restaurants. Eat the most delicious food in the world. Study cooking with the most interesting chefs of France.
Length of trip: 15 days. Group size: 14–18
Cost: $4,500

3. American
California's America fastest, most exciting rivers to raft. You wi The trip is for advent You must be in good
Length of trip: 3 da
Cost: $650

Practicing the Writing Process

A narrative is a story. It tells about a series of actions. Most often the simple past tense is used. Read the student's story about her parents meeting and marrying. Then follow the steps of the writing process.

> My father met my mother in 1980. They met at a college dance. My father liked my mother right away, but my mother did not like my father. He asked her to go out on a date. She wanted to say no, but she was too polite and so she said yes. On their date they went to the movies and saw *Raging Bull*, a movie starring Robert De Niro. After the movie they talked for a long time; they even argued about the movie (he liked it but she didn't). My mother decided that my father was very intelligent. Then my mother started to become interested in him. Soon they were in love.

1 **Exploring Ideas: Free Writing.** Write for ten minutes about how you met someone close to you; or tell about how your parents met. Don't worry about spelling or grammar.

Now tell a partner about your story. Don't read your freewrite aloud. Use your own words.

2 **Writing the First Draft.** Write a first draft of your narrative.

3 **Editing.** Now check your story. Here is a list of things to check for in your narrative.

Editing Checklist

Are the verbs you used transitive or intransitive?

Do any of the verbs have direct objects? Indirect objects? Both? Are these verbs used correctly?

Did you use the simple past tense? (Remember that most often the simple past tense is used in narratives.)

Do you have interesting details in your narrative?

Do your sentences begin with capital letters?

Do other words in the writing need capital letters?

Do your sentences end with periods or other final punctuation?

Make a group with three other students. Take turns and read your story to the others in your group.

4 **Writing the Second Draft.** Write your second draft and give it to your teacher.

Practicing the Writing Process encourages thoughtful composition by guiding students step-by-step from exploring topics to self-editing.

Groupwork maximizes opportunities for discussion and negotiation.

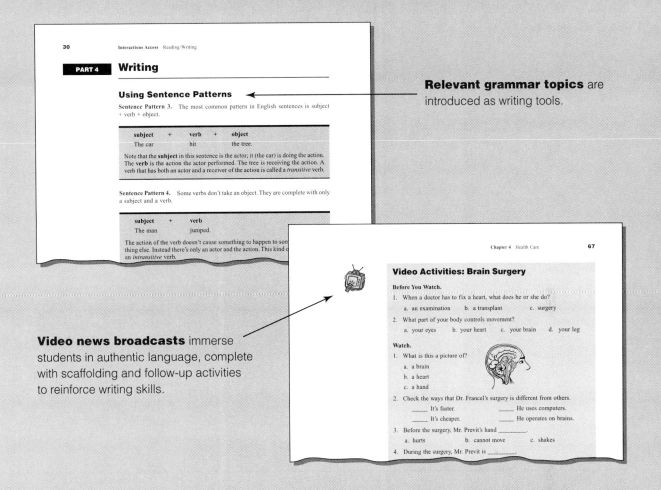

Relevant grammar topics are introduced as writing tools.

Video news broadcasts immerse students in authentic language, complete with scaffolding and follow-up activities to reinforce writing skills.

Don't forget to check out the new *Interactions Mosaic* Website at www.mhcontemporary.com/interactionsmosaic.

- ■ Traditional practice and interactive activities
- ■ Links to student and teacher resources
- ■ Cultural activities
- ■ Focus on Testing
- ■ Activities from the Website are also provided on CD-ROM

Reading Skills/Strategies	Writing Structures	Real-Life Reading/Writing	Video Topics
■ Previewing vocabulary ■ Identifying main ideas ■ Making predictions ■ Following textbook directions	■ *There is/are* ■ *To be* + complement ■ Capital letters and punctuation	■ Post office address form	■ Venice
■ Previewing vocabulary ■ Identifying main ideas ■ Identifying essay organization	■ *Going-to* future ■ Irregular past tense ■ Synopses ■ Quotation marks ■ Textbook directions ■ Transitive vs. intransitive verbs	■ Websites ■ Journal entry	■ Online Pharmacies
■ Previewing vocabulary ■ Identifying main ideas ■ Making predictions	■ Pronoun reference ■ Simple present tense ■ Third-person singular endings	■ Housing ads and telephone bills ■ Journal entry	■ Pet Behavior
■ Previewing vocabulary ■ Identifying main ideas	■ Modals + verb ■ Recognizing paragraph structure	■ Greeting cards ■ Medicine dosage directions	■ Brain Surgery
■ Previewing vocabulary ■ Identifying main ideas ■ Making predictions ■ Reading in phrases	■ Synopses ■ Direct vs. indirect objects ■ *Tell, say, talk*	■ Invitations ■ Thank-you notes ■ Journal entry	■ Women's Football

(continued on next page)

Reading Skills/Strategies	Writing Structures	Real-Life Reading/Writing	Video Topics
■ Previewing vocabulary ■ Identifying main ideas	■ Negative prefixes ■ Past continuous tense ■ Time words ■ Infinitives and gerunds after verbs ■ Linking verbs	■ Journal entry	■ Children and Sleep
■ Previewing vocabulary ■ Identifying main ideas ■ Making predictions	■ Suffix -less ■ Irregular past tense	■ Solicitations for volunteers ■ Résumé ■ Journal entry	■ Dentist Fashion Designer
■ Previewing vocabulary ■ Identifying main ideas	■ Suffix -able ■ Recognizing paragraph structure ■ Command form of verbs	■ Nutrition chart ■ Height/weight chart	■ Diets
■ Previewing vocabulary ■ Identifying main ideas ■ Making predictions	■ Go + ing ■ Adjectives ■ Present, present continuous, past tenses	■ Subway map ■ Journal entry	■ Cancun
■ Previewing vocabulary ■ Identifying main ideas	■ Prefix over- ■ Problem-solution composition	■ Recycling chart ■ Pie chart	■ Recycling

Chapter 1

Neighborhoods, Cities, and Towns

IN THIS CHAPTER

You will read about some problems in very big cities. You will also read about a student's neighborhood, and you will write about your neighborhood.

PART 1   # Monster Cities

Before You Read

1 Discuss the answers to these questions with a partner or a group.

1. Is this city large or small? Is it nice?
2. What is the problem with this city?
3. Do you like cities?

2 **Vocabulary Preview.** It is not always necessary to use a dictionary to find the meaning of a new word. Sometimes the meaning of a new word is after the word *is* or *are* in the sentence.

Example

Population is the number of people in a city or country.

What is population? *the number of people in a city or country*

Answer the questions.

1. A monster is a big, terrible thing.

   What is a monster? _____

2. A megacity is a very, very large city.

   What is a megacity? _____

3. Density is the number of people in a square mile.

   What is density? _____

Read

3 Read the following article quickly. Then do the exercises.

Monster Cities

[A] Are big cities wonderful places? Are they terrible? There are different ideas about this. William H. Whyte writes books about cities. He is happy in a crowded city. He loves busy streets with many stores and many people. He likes the life in city parks and restaurants.

[B]   Many people don't like big cities. They see the large population of cities, and they are afraid. Many cities are growing very fast. They are "monster" cities. (A monster is a big, terrible thing.) In some countries, there aren't jobs in small towns. People go to cities to work; 300,000 people go to São Paulo, Brazil, every year. These cities are megalopolises. A megalopolis is a very large city. But now there is a new word in English—megacity. A megacity is a very, very large city. Mexico City is a megacity with a population of more than 20,000,000. Tokyo-Yokohama is another megacity, with almost 30,000,000 people.

[C]   There are problems in all cities. There are big problems in a megalopolis or megacity. In U.S. cities, there are many people with no jobs and no homes. The air is dirty. There are too many cars. A terrible problem is crime. Many people are afraid of crime.

[D]   Population density is a big problem in megacities. Density is the number of people in an average square mile. In Seoul, South Korea, there are 45,953 people per square mile. Is this crowded? Yes! But in Teheran, Iran, there are 79,594 per square mile. Do you think William H. Whyte likes Hong Kong? The population density there is 247,004!

After You Read

4   **Finding the Main Ideas.**   Complete the sentences. Circle a letter for each blank.

1. "Monster Cities" is about _____.

   a. the large number of small cities

   b. the number of people in U.S. cities

   (c.) the problems of megacities

2. Mexico City, Teheran, and Hong Kong are three _____.

   a. small cities

   b. very big, crowded cities

   c. cities with no crime or dirty air

5   **Making Good Guesses.**   Circle the letter to complete the sentence.

The word *monster* is in the title ("Monster Cities") because _____.

a. the writer is happy in big cities

b. some cities are growing too fast

c. there are people with no jobs and no homes

Discussing the Reading

6   Read the population chart with a partner. Then answer the questions together.

Population of Large Cities			
City, Country	1995	2000	Density*
Tokyo-Yokohama, Japan	28,447,000	29,971,000	24,463
Mexico City, Mexico	23,913,000	27,872,000	37,314
São Paulo, Brazil	21,539,000	25,354,000	38,528
Seoul, South Korea	19,065,000	21,976,000	45,953
New York, USA	14,638,000	14,648,000	11,473
Teheran, Iran	11,681,000	14,251,000	79,594
Jakarta, Indonesia	11,151,000	12,804,000	122,033
Los Angeles, USA	10,414,000	10,714,000	8,985
Hong Kong	5,841,000	5,956,000	247,004
* Population per square mile			

1. What is the population of Tokyo-Yokohama?

2. What is the population of São Paulo, Brazil?

3. What is the population of Mexico City?

4. What is the population density of Los Angeles, USA?

5. What is the population density of Seoul, South Korea?

6. What is the population density of Teheran, Iran?

7. What is the population density of Hong Kong?

8. What is the population of Hong Kong?

9. What is the population density of Jakarta, Indonesia?

Is your city large or small? What is the population? What is nice about your city? What is a problem in your city? Do you like your city? Why or why not?

| PART 2 | # My Neighborhood in the United States |

Before You Read

1 **Making Predictions.** Look at the picture. What kind of neighborhood is this? What country is it in?

Read

2 Read the following article quickly. Then do the exercises.

My Neighborhood in the United States

[A]   My name is Etsuko Sasaki. I'm from Japan, but now I live in California. I'm a student here in English language classes at a small college.

[B]   I live in an apartment building. It's on the corner of Olive Street and Sycamore Avenue. There's a big olive tree in front of the building. There's a park across the street. There are a lot of sycamore trees in the park. The trees are beautiful in the summer.

[C]   A lot of my neighbors are from different countries. The people next to my building are from Indonesia. The family across from the Indonesians is from Colombia.

[D]   The stores in this neighborhood are always busy. There's a Korean drugstore and an Armenian flower shop. A Chinese church is next to the flower shop. There are three restaurants on Olive Street: one Mexican, one Japanese, and one Moroccan-Italian-American!

[E]   I like my neighborhood, but there is one problem. Where are the Americans?

Cross-Cultural Note

Many large cities in North America have neighborhoods with many people from other countries. Two examples in New York City are Chinatown and Little Italy. Do large cities in your home country have different neighborhoods? What kinds of people live in these neighborhoods?

After You Read

3 Read Etsuko's story again. Then look at the map of her neighborhood. Answer the question about it.

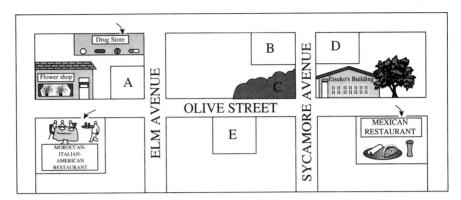

Where are these places? Write the letters from the map on the lines.

  _D_   Indonesian family's house

  _____   Japanese restaurant

  _____   Chinese church

  _____   park

  _____   Colombian family's house

4 **Following Directions.** Read the following directions from textbook exercises. Then follow the directions below.

Directions	**Examples**
1. Circle the word.	(building)
2. Copy the word.	street _street_
3. Underline the word.	<u>building</u>
4. Circle the letter of the answer.	Country:
	a. summer
	(b.) Japan
	c. park
5. Fill in the blank.	My name _is_ Etsuko.
6. Write the word on the line	_neighborhood_
7. Correct the mistake.	co^r^ner

Now follow these directions.

1. Circle the name of a city.

   Brazil   Indonesia   Tokyo   Egypt

2. Copy the name of a person.

   Mexico _____   California _____

   the USA _____   Etsuko _____

3. Underline the word for a building.

   I'm at a restaurant now.

4. Circle the letter of a kind of restaurant in Etsuko's neighborhood.

   a. Chinese   b. Mexican   c. Korean   d. Indonesian

5. Write the name of your country on the line. _____

6. Correct the mistake.

   colombia

5 **Building Vocabulary.** Write the words from the box on the correct lines.

church	Colombia	apartment building	Japan
Italian	Mexican	flower shop	Korean
restaurant	Indonesian	Moroccan	Armenian
Indonesia	drugstore	olive	Japanese
sycamore	American		

Countries   _Indonesia_____

Trees   _sycamore_____

Person (or thing) From a Country   _Italian_____

Buildings   _church_____

Fill each blank with a word from the box.

front	crowded	different	next	building	neighbors

1. This store is always _____. There are always lots and lots of people.

2. There is a big apartment _____ on the corner.

3. There is a school _____ to my house.

4. My _____ are from Mexico. They're nice people.

5. There are two big trees in _____ of my house.

6. People in my neighborhood are from _____ countries.

Discussing the Reading

6 Answer the questions. Then discuss your answers with a group.

1. What stores are in your neighborhood?
2. Are there people from different countries in your neighborhood? What countries are they from?
3. Draw a map of your neighborhood. Describe the map to the other members of your group.

PART 3   A Post Office Address Form

Here is a change of address form. It's from the post office. When you move to a new house, apartment, or business in the United States, you need to complete a change of address form from the post office.

As soon as you know your new address, mail this card to all of the people, businesses, and publications who send you mail.

For publications, tape an old address label over name and old address sections and complete new address.

Your Name (Print or type. Last name, first name, middle initial.)

ANDERSON, PAUL

Old Address

No. & Street	Apt./Suite No.	PO Box	RR No.	Rural Box No.
96 SYCAMORE AVE.				

City	State	ZIP + 4
SANTA ROSA	CA	90012-3362

New Address

No. & Street	Apt./Suite No.	PO Box	RR No.	Rural Box No.
8962 ELM ST.				

City	State	ZIP + 4
GREENWICH	CT	06839-0118

Sign Here	Date new address in effect	Keyline No. (If any)
Paul Anderson	12/04/01	

PS Form **3576**, November 1990   RECEIVER: Be sure to record the above new address.

Circle a letter to complete each sentence.

1. The new address is for _____.

   a. one person   b. a family   c. a store

2. The new house is in the city of _____.

   a. California   b. Santa Rosa   c. Greenwich

3. The person wants to receive mail at the new house on _____.

   a. December 4, 2001   b. April 12, 2000   c. Dec. 12, 2000

PART 4	# Writing

Read this student's description of a favorite place.

My Favorite Place

I live in Los Angeles. My favorite place is near there. The name of the place is the Huntington Library and Gardens. There are many different kinds of gardens there. There is a Japanese garden, a desert garden, a rose garden, an Australian garden, and many others. My favorite garden is the rose garden.

There are almost 1500 kinds of rose bushes in the garden. In the summer, many of them have flowers. There are roses from the 1600s to modern times, and there are red roses, pink roses, and roses of every other color. The garden is full of the smell of roses. The grass is very soft and green. Sometimes there is the sound of the big bell in the Japanese garden, and there are always the sounds of birds and trees.

The garden is a beautiful place.

Using Sentence Patterns

Sentence Pattern 1.   When we describe a place, we use basic sentence patterns over and over. We use *there is/are* in this way.

there is/ there are	+	noun phrase	+	prepositional phrase (optional)
There is		a rose bush		in the garden.

Good descriptions always have details. Details are specific facts. General statements are often boring. Details are interesting.

General Statement	**Detail or Fact**
There are many kinds of roses in the garden.	There are almost 1500 different kinds of rose bushes in the garden.
There are nice sounds.	There are always the sounds of the birds and the leaves in the trees.

Look at the preceding description of the Huntington Gardens. Complete this chart using sentences from the description.

There is/There are	noun phrase	adverb or prepositional phrase
There are	many different kinds of gardens	there.
	a Japanese garden, a desert garden, a rose garden, an Australian garden, and many others.	X
		in the garden.
There are		X
	red roses, pink roses, and roses of every other color.	X
		in the Japanese garden.
There are always		X

Sentence Pattern 2.   The verb *to be* is often followed by complements.

subject	+	be	+	complement
I		am		from Japan.

Sometimes the complement is a prepositional phrase.

A lot of my neighbors	are	from different countries.

Sometimes the complement is an adjective (a word that describes the subject).

The stores	are	busy.
The grass	is	very soft and green.

A paragraph is a group of sentences. The sentences are about the same idea. A paragraph always begins with an indented space. Read this paragraph and complete the chart.

indented space → I am a student. I live in Los Angeles. My favorite place is near there. The name of the place is the Huntington Library and Gardens. The library is a beautiful white building. In spring the gardens are full of flowers. There are many visitors then.

subject	be	complement
I	am	a student.
	is	near there.
The name of the place		
		a beautiful white building.
In spring the gardens		

Practicing the Writing Process

Writers do not sit down and write something perfect the first time. There are steps:

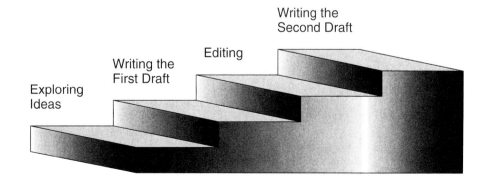

1 **Exploring Ideas: Brainstorming.** Think about your favorite place. Write down at least six sentences telling about that place. Begin your sentences with *there is* or *there are.*

1. There is/are _____.

2. _____

3. _____

4. _____

5. _____

6. _____

Now tell a partner or the members of your group about your favorite place but don't read your sentences aloud. Sometimes talking about your writing helps improve it.

2 **Writing the First Draft.** A draft is when you practice or try writing something. Write a paragraph about your favorite place. Use Sentence Patterns 1 and 2. Remember to include details.

3 **Editing.** Good writers never write only one draft. They write, then edit—correct their work and make changes, then write at least a second draft. (Some writers write five or ten drafts!) Here are some things to look for when you edit:

Using Capital Letters and Correct Punctuation

■ Every sentence begins with a capital letter and ends with a period, exclamation mark, or question mark.

 This is my neighborhood.
 ^   ^
 capital   period

■ There is a comma between a city and state or a city and country.

 San Francisco, California
 Jakarta, Indonesia
        ^
    comma

■ These words have a capital letter.

names of cities	São Paulo
names of states	Texas
names of countries	Iran
person or thing from a country	American, Korean
languages	Japanese
street names	Olive Street, Sycamore Avenue
people's names	Etsuko Sasaki
names of stores, buildings, and parks	Han's Drugstore
the word "I"	

Correct the mistakes.

> my favorite place is my grandmother's house she lives in new jersey near new york city there is a rose garden behind her house and there is also a small river in the summer there is the sound of the water and the smell of the roses the river is cool and fresh

Now check the first draft of your paragraph about your favorite place. Use the following checklist to correct any mistakes.

Editing Checklist

Do your sentences begin with capital letters?
Do other words in your paragraph need capital letters?
Do your sentences end with periods?
Do any words in your paragraph need a comma between them?

Show your paragraph to another student. Read each other's paragraphs and discuss each other's work. Are there interesting details? Are the descriptions clear? Use the editing list to check your classmate's paragraph.

4 **Writing the Second Draft.** Now you are ready to write your second draft. When you are finished, give it to your teacher.

Video Activities: Venice

Before You Watch.

1. Where is the city of Venice? Circle the correct answer.

    a. France   b. Italy   c. Greece

2. Venice is famous because it has

    a. old buildings.   b. many canals.   c. a lot of rain.

Watch. Check all the correct answers.

> Vocabulary Note:
> *To sink* means to go under the water. The past tense is *sank*.

1. What are Venice's problems?

   _____ The canals are crowded.

   _____ The water is very dirty.

   _____ There is a lot of air pollution.

   _____ No one wants to go there.

   _____ It is sinking.

2. Venice needs

   _____ money.

   _____ tourists.

   _____ water.

Watch Again.

1. Complete the sentences with numbers from the box.

200	30	6,000,000	1

  1. Venice has about _____ canals.

  2. A few years ago Venice sank about _____ foot.

  3. They cleaned the canals _____ years ago.

  4. About _____ tourists visit Venice each year.

2. Bob Guthrie's group is called "_____ Venice."

  a. Visit   b. Stop   c. Save

After You Watch. Each sentence in this paragraph has a grammatical error. Find the errors and rewrite the paragraph correctly.

Venice is Italy. It very old city. Has many canals. Venice have many problems too. There a lot of air pollution and water pollution. There are a lot of tourist in Venice too. The government of Italy has not money for Venice's problems.

Chapter 2

Shopping and e-Commerce

IN THIS CHAPTER

You will read about shopping on the Internet. You will also read about predicting the future, and you will write a prediction—a description of an imaginary new product or invention.

| PART 1 |

Shopping on the Internet

Before You Read

1 Discuss the following questions with a partner or a group.

1. Do you have a computer? Do any of your friends have computers?
2. Do you use the Internet? Do any of your friends use the Internet?
3. Did you know about the Internet two years ago? Five years ago? Ten years ago?
4. Do you shop on the Internet? What do you buy on the Internet?

2 **Vocabulary Preview.**   Sometimes a dictionary isn't necessary to find the meaning of a new word. The meaning is sometimes in parentheses ( ).

Example

Many people are <u>online</u> (using the Internet).

What is *online*? _using the Internet_

Write the meaning of the underlined word on the line.

1. Amazon.com has 10 million <u>customers</u> (people who buy things).

   What are customers? _____

2. You can visit <u>virtual</u> (not real) shopping malls online.

   What is *virtual?* _____

3. They sell <u>home improvement products</u> (things you use to fix up a house).

   What is a home improvement product? _____

   _____

3 **Making Good Guesses.**   Circle the letter to complete the sentence.

1. We bought the house for $100,000. We sold it for $110,000. We made a $10,000 <u>profit</u>.

    A <u>profit</u> is most likely _____.

    a. money you lose in business

    b. money you make in business

    c. money you pay for a house

2. Jeff Bezos had very little money. The company began in a <u>garage</u>, and at first there were very few customers.

    A <u>garage</u> is most likely a _____.

    a. big, expensive house

    b. place to play baseball

    c. small, inexpensive building

4 **Using Verbs.**   We can use *(be) going to* to talk about the future. (Note that *going to* is often pronounced "gonna" in relaxed speech.)

Subject	Future Form	Verb Phrase
The Internet	is going to	continue to grow.
People	are going to	shop online.

Write a sentence with *going to*. Share it with a partner.

Many common verbs are irregular in the past tense. Do you know the verbs in the box? Work with a partner. Use some of the verbs in sentences. Use both tenses.

Present Tense	Past Tense
know	knew
is	was
have	had
quit	quit
drive	drove
begin	began
sell	sold
think	thought

Read

5 Read the article. Don't use your dictionary. If you don't know some words, try to figure out their meaning.

Internet Shopping

[A] Twenty years ago very few people used the Internet. Only scientists and people in the government knew about the Internet and how to use it. This is changing very fast. Now almost everyone knows about the Internet, and many people are online (using the Internet) every day. When people think about the Internet, they often think about information. But now, more and more, when people think about the Internet, they think about shopping.

[B]   Amazon.com was one of the first companies to try to sell products on the Internet. Jeff Bezos started the company. He was a successful vice-president of a company in New York. One day he had a vision of the future. He thought, "The World Wide Web is growing 2000 percent a year. It's going to continue to grow. Shopping is going to move to the Internet. People are going to shop online." He quit his good job and drove across the country to Seattle, Washington. There he started an online bookstore called Amazon.com. Bezos had very little money. The company began in a garage, and at first there were very few customers (people who buy things).

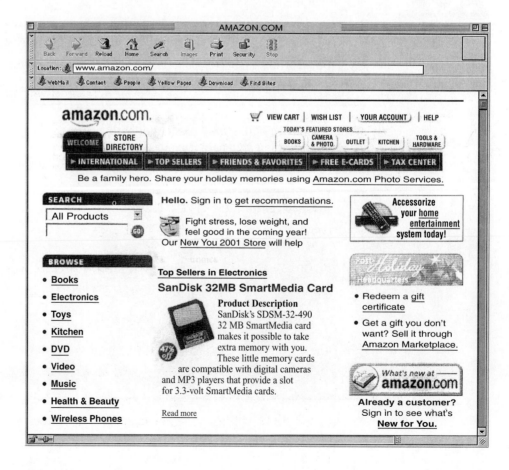

[C]   At the Amazon.com site, people can search for a book about a subject, find many different books about that subject, read what other people think about the books, order them by credit card, and get them in the mail in two days. This kind of bookstore was a new idea, but the business grew. In a few years, Amazon.com had 10 million customers and listed (sold) 18 million different items in categories including books, CDs, toys, electronics, videos, DVDs, home improvement products (things you use to fix up a house), software, and video games. Today you can buy anything from gourmet food to caskets at a "virtual shopping mall," that is, a group of stores all over the world that functions like a group of stores all in one place.

Jeff Bezos

[D]   Are people going to shop online more and more? No one knows for sure. Online shopping is growing, but it may not make money for companies like Amazon.com. Jeff Bezos is a billionaire, but his billions of dollars are invested in the company; even after several years, Amazon.com was still not making a profit. If online shopping continues to grow, Bezos hopes his investment will produce real profits.

After You Read

6   **Finding the Main Ideas.**   Circle the letter to complete the sentence.

1. The title of the article is "Internet Shopping." Another possible title is _____.

    a. "Internet Games"

    b. "Shopping on the Internet"

    c. "Information and the Internet"

2. The main idea of Paragraph A is _____.

    a. Nowadays more and more people use the Internet, especially to shop

    b. Twenty years ago very few people used the Internet

    c. Scientists were first to use the Internet

3. The main idea of Paragraph B is _____.

    a. The Web is growing 2000 percent a year

    b. Amazon.com is an example of a company that sells on the Internet

    c. Jeff Bezos quit his good job and moved to Seattle, Washington

4. The main idea of Paragraph C is _____.

   a. People can order books by credit card

   b. Amazon.com grew

   c. People can search for a book on Amazon.com

5. The main idea of Paragraph D is _____.

   a. Online shopping is going to grow

   b. Jeff Bezos is a billionaire

   c. Online shopping may or may not grow

Organizing a Reading

"Internet Shopping" is a typical information article. The organization is very simple:

1. Introduction of the subject (Paragraph A)
2. A good example (Paragraph B)
3. More details of that example (Paragraph C)
4. Conclusion (Paragraph D)

Synopsis

You can say the main information in "Internet Shopping" in a short paragraph. This is called a *synopsis*. A synopsis gives the main ideas of a reading or an article. Here is a synopsis of "Internet Shopping."

Many people are now shopping on the Internet. One example is the online bookstore Amazon.com. Amazon.com has a lot of customers, but it is not making a profit yet. No one knows the future of online shopping.

Understanding Quotation Marks

We use quotation marks to tell what someone says or thinks. For example:

He thought, "The World Wide Web is growing 2000 percent a year."

Discussing the Reading

7 Discuss the following questions with a group or a partner. Then share your answers with the class.

1. Do any of your friends spend a lot of time online? Is this good or bad?

2. Some people even shop for food on the Internet. Do you think Internet shopping is going to get bigger and more important in your country? How big and how important is it going to get?

| **PART 2** | **Predicting the Future** |

Before You Read

1 Look at the photos. Discuss with a partner or group what is happening in each one.

2 **Vocabulary Preview.** Sometimes the meaning of a word is after a dash (—) or between two dashes.

Example

Predicting the future—telling what is going to happen in the future—is a very difficult thing to do.

What does *predicting* mean?

Telling people what is going to happen in the future.

Answer the questions.

1. Microchips—the most important part of a computer—are getting smaller and smaller.

    What is a microchip?

    _____

2. Every family will have a robot—a smart machine—to clean their house and take care of them.

    What is a robot?

    _____

3. Global warming is going to cause many large cities to flood—they are going to be under water.

    What does *flood* mean?

    _____

If you don't know a word, you can sometimes guess the meaning from examples. Often these examples follow the words *such as*.

Example

He likes fruit *such as* apples, oranges, and grapes.

What are some examples of fruit? _apples, oranges, and grapes_

Answer the questions.

1. There are still serious diseases such as cancer, TB, AIDS, and cholera.

    What are some examples of diseases?

    _____

2. The children have many toys in their room such as little trucks, balls, dolls, and plastic airplanes.

    What are some examples of toys?

    _____

3. Some people have all kinds of digital equipment such as computers, cameras, and DVD players.

    What are some examples of digital equipment?

    _____

4. The movies have many famous actors such as Matt Dillon, Bruce Willis, and Julia Roberts.

    Who are some actors?

    _____

Read

3   Read the article. Don't use your dictionary. If you don't know some words, try to guess their meaning.

Predicting the Future

[A]   Predicting the future—telling what is going to happen in the future—is a very difficult thing to do. Some people, like Jeff Bezos, are able to somehow "see the future" and know what is going to happen next and what to do as a result. Most people, even very smart people, have a hard time doing this. For example, here are some famous predictions from the past.

[B]   "I think companies are going to sell maybe five computers."
—computer company executive, 1943

"No one is going to want a computer in their home."
—president of a large computer company, 1977

"Who wants to hear actors talk?"
—movie company executive, 1927

"Airplanes are interesting toys but they have no military use."
—French professor of war, 1910

"Man is never going to reach the moon."
—inventor and scientist, 1952

"For most people, smoking is good for their health."
—a doctor, quoted in a national magazine, 1963

"But what is a microchip good for?"
—a computer engineer, 1968

---

4   Here are some predications about the next 50 years. Do you agree with them?

1. Every family will have a robot—a smart machine—to clean their house and take care of them.
2. Scientists are going to have a cure for cancer in ten years.
3. Everyone in the world is going to use the Internet every day.
4. The world is going to become very hot because of pollution and "global warming." This is going to flood many large cities—they are going to be under water.
5. A very bad disease is going to kill 50 percent of all human beings.
6. No one is going to read books or magazines—they are going to listen to them on digital equipment.
7. No one in the world is going to smoke cigarettes.
8. Religion is going to become more important for people.
9. Everyone in the world is going to speak English as a first or second language.
10. China is going to be the richest country in the world.

After You Read

5   **Stating Opinions.** The word *likely* means "probably" or "possibly." We can use this word to state an opinion about a prediction.

very likely	(I think this is going to happen.)
fairly likely	(I think this may happen.)
not very likely	(I don't think this is going to happen.)
not likely	(This is not going to happen.)

Think about the ten predictions in the preceding exercise. Then write your opinion—"very likely," "fairly likely," "not very likely," or "not likely" next to the number of the prediction in the following list.

1. _____

2. _____

3. _____

4. _____

5. _____

6. _____

7. _____

8. _____

9. _____

10. _____

Now talk with a partner or a group and share your answers. Were your answers the same or different? Discuss your answers. Give reasons for your choices.

Discussing the Reading

6   Read the article again. What are the quotations (the things the different people said) in part B about? What do the different persons really mean?

Example

"I think companies are going to sell maybe five computers."

This person thinks that computers will never become popular.
Discuss the meanings with a partner. Then share your ideas with a group.

7   **Following Directions.**   Match the words. Write letters on the lines.

1. __f__ future   a. television
2. _____ billion   b. flower
3. _____ cancer   c. customer
4. _____ garden   d. dollars
5. _____ actor   e. disease
6. _____ shopping   f. prediction

Match the words. Draw lines.

1. the Internet   a. the number of people in a square mile
2. density   b. fixing up a house
3. monster   c. the Web
4. garage   d. no space
5. crowded   e. like real but on a computer
6. home improvement   f. a terrible thing
7. virtual   g. a place to keep cars

An adjective is a word that tells us information about a noun—for example, *big* is an adjective in "a big house." Put a check next to the adjectives in the following list.

1. __✔__ smart   5. _____ free
2. _____ virtual   6. _____ information
3. _____ clean   7. _____ good
4. _____ fruit

| PART 3 | # Einstein and the Internet |

1 Look at the photo. Do you know this person? Who is he? Can you explain his theory?

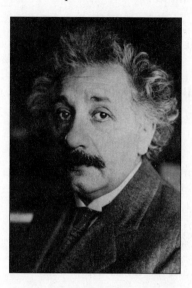

2 Read the information. Then do the exercises.

Searching the Internet

To search for information on the Internet, you begin by typing in a key word or name such as "Einstein" on your computer. Then you get a list of Websites. You have to scan the list—read through it quickly—to try to find the important sites for you. Don't try to understand every word—you only need to know what the different sites are basically about. When you click on a Website listing, you get the actual Website or Webpage. This is where you find more complete information about your key word or name, including many details and often photos, diagrams, and pictures.

Here are some words and phrases from Website listings for "Einstein." How many of the following words do you know? From these words, can you guess what the site is about? Work in a group and discuss your answers.

1. letters and writings
2. Harvard University
3. sales, equipment, supplies
4. game
5. synopsis

6. videos
7. kids, high school
8. cancer, hospital
9. Massachusetts Institute of Technology

If you don't know the meaning of these words, look at the end of this chapter.

Now read the following Website listings.

Write the number of the preceding Website above that is <u>best</u> for your needs in the blank that says "first choice _____." Write the number of the <u>second best</u> site in the blank that says "second choice _____."

1. You are doing homework for science class about Einstein.

    first choice _____   second choice _____

2. You are reading a book and you want some general information to help you understand Einstein's life and theories.

    first choice _____   second choice _____

3. You are a scientist. You understand Einstein very well but you want some new or more detailed information about him.

    first choice _____   second choice _____

4. You're looking for scientific equipment and you remember a good supply company. You think its name has Einstein in it.

    first choice _____   second choice _____

Discuss your answers with a group. Did all group members pick the same choices? Why or why not?

PART 4

Writing

Using Sentence Patterns

Sentence Pattern 3.   The most common pattern in English sentences is subject + verb + object.

subject	+	verb	+	object
The car		hit		the tree.

Note that the **subject** in this sentence is the actor; it (the car) is doing the action. The **verb** is the action the actor performed. The tree is receiving the action. A verb that has both an actor and a receiver of the action is called a *transitive* verb.

Sentence Pattern 4.   Some verbs don't take an object. They are complete with only a subject and a verb.

subject	+	verb
The man		jumped.

The action of the verb doesn't cause something to happen to someone or something else. Instead there's only an actor and the action. This kind of verb is called an *intransitive* verb.

With intransitive verbs, there is often a prepositional phrase after the verb that tells us where, when, or how the action happened.

subject	+	verb	+	prepositional phrase
The man		jumped		in the pool.

Note that many verbs can be both transitive and intransitive.

Do the following sentences use Sentence Pattern 3 or 4? Write 3 or 4 in the space.

1. __3__ Fifteen or twenty years ago very few people used the Internet.

2. _____ But his business grew.

3. _____ Bezos had a vision of the future.

4. _____ He quit his good job.

5. _____ He started an online bookstore called Amazon.com.

6. _____ The company began in a garage.

7. _____ The World Wide Web is growing.

8. _____ Some people don't like this idea.

Practicing the Writing Process

Read a student's prediction of a new plant.

> A new plant is going to be very popular. It is called a *tomana*. It is a combination of a tomato and a banana. The tomana looks like a red banana but it smells like a tomato. The outside peel (skin) is very thick and protects the fruit inside. It is easy to peel the tomana. When you remove the peel, you have a perfect tomato/banana. It is easy to slice the peeled tomana for salads or sandwiches.

1 **Exploring Ideas: Free Writing.** One way to get ideas is to "freewrite." When you freewrite, you write for ten minutes about your idea. Do not worry about your spelling or grammar. Just try to get a lot of ideas down. Your teacher does not correct or look at a freewrite. The purpose of a freewrite is simply to help you get ideas. Sometimes if you can't think of anything to say, just write "I can't think of anything to say" many times. The main thing is to keep on writing. For example, you can write about a new combination of two fruits or vegetables, like the *tomana* in the student's prediction. What does the new fruit/vegetable look like? What does it smell like? What does it taste like? Or write about a new machine of the future that does some difficult job. What does it do? What does it look like?

Now tell a partner or a group about your prediction. Don't read your freewrite aloud but use the ideas from it.

When we want to describe someone or something, we often make a comparison between the two persons or things. To do so, we often use a verb of perception (smell, feel, look, sound, taste) with the word *like*:

Example

My brother looks *like* my sister.

Think about your prediction. Can you complete this sentence about it?

It looks like _____

_____.

What does it smell like? What does it sound, feel, or taste like?

2 **Writing the First Draft.** Now write the first draft of your prediction.

3   **Editing.**   After writing your first draft, it's time to edit your work. Here is a checklist of things to look for in your paragraph.

Editing Checklist

Do your sentences begin with capital letters?

Do other words in your paragraph need capital letters?

Do your sentences end with periods or other final punctuation?

Do any words in your paragraph need a comma after them?

Are the words spelled correctly? (Use your dictionary!)

Do you have interesting details?

Show your paragraph to a partner. Read each other's paragraphs. Are there interesting details? Is the description clear?

4   **Writing the Second Draft.**   Now write the second draft of your prediction. Then give it to your teacher.

Writing a Journal

Write a journal entry about your plans for the future. Use *going to* and the past tense verbs in Part 1 if you can.

> I'm going to study chemistry. I want to be a chemist.
>
> My sister is going to study medicine. She wants to be a doctor.

Word Meanings from Page 28 [Einstein Website terms]:

1. Writings are the books and papers someone wrote during his or her life.
2. Harvard University is one of the best and most famous universities in the United States.
3. *Sales* means selling things. Equipment and supplies are things you use to do something—for example, a paper, pen, and books are supplies for a student.
4. A game is something you play for fun—for example, baseball or computer games.
5. A synopsis is a short statement of the important ideas of a paragraph or longer writing.
6. Videos are tapes you can watch on a television.
7. *Kids* is a slang term for "young people." High school is where students study after elementary school.
8. Cancer is a disease. A hospital is a place for sick people.
9. The Massachusetts Institute of Technology is near Harvard in Cambridge, Massachusetts. It is one of the best universities for science in the United States.

Video Activities: Online Pharmacies

Before You Watch.

1. Which of these stores sell medicine?

   a. a pharmacy   b. a bakery   c. a hardware store

2. What is a prescription?

   a. a kind of medicine

   b. doctor's permission to buy a type of medicine

Watch.

1. What is the message of this video?

   a. Don't buy drugs online.

   b. Be careful when you buy drugs online.

   c. Always buy drugs online.

2. What is happening to drug sales on the Internet?

   a. More and more people are buying drugs online.

   b. Not many people are buying drugs online.

   c. Online pharmacies are not popular.

Watch Again.

1. Complete the following chart.

   Sale of Drugs Online

Year	Amount
2000	$ _____
2001	$ 400,000,000
_____	$ 1,100,000,000
2003	$ _____
_____	$ _____

2. Check the benefits of buying drugs online.

   _____ accountability   _____ convenience

   _____ price   _____ privacy

   _____ reliability   _____ safety

After You Watch.   Write a paragraph about shopping online. Do you think online shopping is a good idea? Why or why not?

Chapter 3

Friends and Family

IN THIS CHAPTER

You will read about changes in families in different countries. You will also read about an American tradition—a family reunion—and you will write a letter about yourself.

PART 1   # Changing Families

Before You Read

1   Look at the photos. Then answer these questions. Make a guess if you aren't sure of the answer.

1.   How many people are in photo 1? Who are they?

2.   How many people are in photo 2? Who are they?

3.   How many people are in photo 3? Who are they?

Photo 1

Photo 3

Photo 2

2 Vocabulary Preview.   Learning words in groups that go together will help you learn vocabulary. For example, *marriage, partnership*, and *union* all mean a kind of "joining together." Answer these questions in small groups.

1. Which word from the group *marriage, partnership, union* would you apply to these situations?

   a. countries that decide to use the same money system
   b. a man and a woman who make a life together
   c. workers from one industry
   d. two women who want to make a life together
   e. two people who start a new business
   f. two men who want to make a life together

2. Which word from the group *family, blended family, extended family* would you apply to these situations?

   a. a man, a woman, their two children, and a nephew that they are raising
   b. a man, a woman, their child
   c. a man with two children who marries a woman with three children
   d. a woman with one child
   e. a man, a woman, their two children, and the man's mother who lives with them
   f. a man and a woman who aren't married but who live together

Read

3 Read the following material quickly. Then do the exercises.

Changing Families

[A] Families in almost every country are changing. In North Africa, in the past, many people lived in extended families. Fifty to a hundred people lived together in a group of houses. These were all family members—grandparents, aunts, uncles, cousins, children, and grandchildren. But now this traditional family is breaking into smaller groups.

[B]   The traditional Japanese family was also an extended family—a son, his parents, his wife, his children, and his unmarried brothers and sisters. They lived together in his parents' home. But this tradition is changing. Now most adults do not live with their parents. They have new problems. Men and women spend a lot of time at work. They don't spend a lot of time together as a family. This can be very difficult.

[C]   In Europe, in traditional families, the woman stayed home with the children and the man had a job. But families all over Europe are changing. The number of divorces is going up. The number of single-parent families is going up too. In Sweden, more than 40 percent (40%) of all children have parents that are not married. More and more countries are recognizing gay partnerships and mar-riages. For example, Denmark, Sweden, Norway, the Netherlands, Hungary, and the U.S. state of Vermont all recognize these as legal unions. In much of Europe, many people live alone. In France, more than 26 percent of women between age 30 and 34 live alone, and more than 27 percent of men of the same age live alone.

[D]   There are also big changes in Quebec, Canada. In 1965, a traditional family was important. Almost 90 percent of men and 93.5 percent of women were married. But in 1985, only 49 percent of men and 51.7 percent of women were married! Now more than one-third (1/3) of all babies have parents that are not married. More than one-third of all marriages end in divorce.

[E]   There are many new types of families. The world is changing, and families are changing too.

After You Read

4 **Finding the Main Ideas.**   Circle a letter for each blank.

1. The main idea is that _____.

    a. in North Africa, families are big, but in Europe, they're small

    b. families around the world are changing

    c. 1/3 of all marriages end in divorce

2. The writer thinks that new families are _____.

    a. good because they are small

    b. different from families in the past

    c. bad because people don't live together

5 **Understanding Pronouns.**   Find and circle the meaning of each underlined pro-noun. Then draw an arrow from the pronoun to its meaning.

1. (Fifty to a hundred people) live together in a group of houses. These are all family members.

2. Men and women spend a lot of time at work. They don't spend a lot of time together as a family.

3. They don't spend a lot of time together as a family. This can be very difficult.

4. More and more countries are recognizing gay partnerships and marriages. For example, Denmark, Sweden, Norway, the Netherlands, Hungary, and the U.S. state of Vermont all recognize these as legal unions.

Discussing the Reading

6   Talk about your answers to these questions with your classmates.

1. What kind of family do you live in?

2. Why are families in some countries smaller than in the past?

3. Why are there more single-parent families now?

PART 2   # Our Family Reunion

Before You Read

1   **Making Predictions.**   Look at the three pictures. Who are these people? What is happening in each picture?

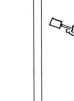

Cross-Cultural Note

In the United States, many people adopt children. (They take children without parents into their home and become their parents.) They often adopt children who are older or who have special needs. Would you rather adopt a baby or an older child? Would you adopt a child with special needs?

a.

b.

c.

Read

2 Read the story. Then do the exercises.

Our Family Reunion

[A] These are pictures of my family. We don't live together. We live in different cities, but we often talk to each other on the phone. Every summer all the relatives come together for a week. This is our family reunion.

[B] In our family, people come to the reunion from Massachusetts, New Mexico, British Columbia, and Louisiana. One of my cousins flies to the United States from Ireland! We usually meet in a small town in Pennsylvania. My great-grandparents lived in this town.

[C] At the reunion, we have a picnic one day at a beautiful lake. We play baseball, swim, and eat a lot. We play volleyball too. The women and girls are on one team, and the men and boys are on the other. One night we always have a big barbecue. We sit around a fire, tell stories, and eat a lot. On the last night, we have a dinner dance at a nice hotel. We listen to music, dance, and eat a lot. Our family really likes to eat.

[D] We don't only eat. We visit with each other all week. We talk about problems. We plan weddings and cry about divorces. Sometimes we argue. All bring their new babies, new wives and husbands, and new girlfriends and boyfriends.

[E] It's good to have a big family. But at the end of the week, I'm always very tired! I'm happy to be alone.

After You Read

3 Answer the following questions about the story. Circle the letters of the answers.

1. How often do the people have a reunion?

   a. each month   b. every year   c. every five years

2. How long is the reunion?

   a. one week   b. two weeks   c. one year

3. What's most important about a family reunion?

   a. It's a chance to eat a lot.

   b. It brings distant family members together.

   c. All bring their new wives.

4. How does the writer feel at the end of the week?

   a. unhappy   b. hungry   c. tired

Cross-Cultural Note

In many families in the United States and Canada, family members live far from each other—in different cities or states—but their friends live nearby. For some of these people, their friends are very, very important. Their friends are almost a second, new "family." Does this sometimes happen in your country?

Dictionary Use—Alphabetizing

Sometimes you need to use a dictionary. The words in a dictionary are in alphabetical order—A to Z. It's important to know how to alphabetize quickly. You need to look at the first letter of each word to put words in alphabetical order.

Example

These words are in alphabetical order.

> **a**lcohol
> **d**iet
> **f**ood
> **w**alk

If the first letter is the same, you need to look at the second letter too.

> **ca**ndy
> **ci**garette
> **cu**p

If the first and second letters are the same, you need to look at the third letter, and so on.

> **cof**fee
> **col**a
> **com**pany

---

4   **Following Directions.**   Finish writing the 26 letters of the English alphabet in order. Write as fast as you can.

 _a_   _b_   ____ ____ ____ ____ ____ ____ ____ ____

 ____ ____ ____ ____ ____ ____ ____ ____ ____

 ____ ____ ____ ____ ____ ____

Put the words in alphabetical order by numbering them. The first word is 1; the second word is 2; and so on.

1. _____ every

   _____ elderly

   _____ exercise

   __1__ eggs

2. _____ golf

   _____ gold

   _____ glass

   _____ gray

3. _____ remember

   _____ relatives

   _____ reusable

   _____ reunion

4. _____ full   _____ environment

   _____ marriage   _____ change

   _____ world   _____ fire

5. _____ together   _____ traditional   _____ guy

   _____ visit   _____ group   _____ very

   _____ trees   _____ volleyball   _____ groceries

6. _____ special   _____ cultural   _____ hotel

   _____ almost   _____ reunion   _____ alone

   _____ cry   _____ aunt   _____ come

   _____ husband   _____ safe   _____ shirt

5 **Building Vocabulary.** Fill in the crossword puzzle with these words from the story.

parent	lot	divorce	fire	far
team	cousin	night	lake	eat
relatives	reunion	aunt	picnic	to

Across

2. a group of people in a game
5. people in your family
7. your mother's or father's sister
8. Sometimes we eat lunch outside. This is a _____.
10. something very hot (we can cook over it)
11. not day
14. a mother or father

Down

1. You can swim in a _____.
3. We need to _____ food every day.
4. the end of a marriage
5. a meeting of people after a long time
6. We eat a _____. (= much)
9. the child of your aunt and uncle
12. Every summer we go _____ a reunion.
13. He lives _____ from here. (= not near)

Discussing the Reading

6   In a small group, talk about families. Ask each person these questions. Fill in the answers on this chart.

Student's Name	Who do you live with?	Where do your relatives live?	How often do you visit your relatives?	Do you have family reunions? When? Where?

PART 3 | **Housing Ads and Telephone Bills**

FURNISHED HOUSE (FURN HOUSE)

UNFURNISHED HOUSE (UNF HOUSE)

pets

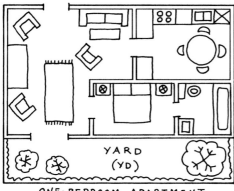

ONE-BEDROOM APARTMENT
(1- BD APT)

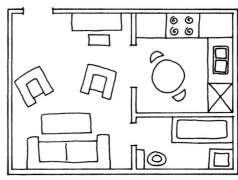

SINGLE APARTMENT (SGL APT)

SECURITY BUILDING
(SEC BLDG)

1 **Understanding Housing Ads.**   Some people look at ads in a newspaper to find a house or apartment to rent. Read about the following people. Which apartment is good for each family or person? On the lines, write the telephone numbers from the ads.

~~rmance & ~~~~m.~~o. B.~
UNF HOUSE
3bd, near schools,
big yard, pets ok
555-3211

FURN APT
1 bd, quiet bldg
555-6138

SGL APT
Furn apt, sec bldg
stv/frig, no pets
555-4826

UNF APT
2 bd, stv/frig,
w/pool 555-9277

FURN HOUSE
3 bd, near bus/
subway 555-6292

Phone Number

1. A woman lives alone, but sometimes she is afraid. She doesn't have furniture. She doesn't have a stove or refrigerator. She doesn't have a dog or cat. _____

2. A man and a woman have two children and a dog. They have furniture. _____

3. A man and a woman have one child. They don't have a stove or refrigerator. They have furniture. All three family members like to swim. _____

4. A young man and a young woman are married, but they don't have children. They are college students. They need to study hard. They don't have furniture. _____

5. Three young men are friends. They are students in an adult school. They also work. They don't have cars or furniture. _____

2 **Reading a Telephone Bill.**   Friends and family members sometimes live far from each other. The telephone is important to them. Look at this telephone bill. Then answer the questions about it with a partner.

PACIFIC ☒ BELL.
A Pacific Telesis Company

Account Number	-4983 362 S 7184	Please Save For Your Records Check No: Date: Amount:		Page 1

Account Summary	Previous bill	45.03	
	Payments applied through Nov 16	45.03CR	
	Balance *** Thank You for Your Payment ***		.00
	Current charges:		
	Pacific Bell (Page 2)	29.21	
	AT&T (Page 4)	5.54	
	CURRENT CHARGES DUE BY Dec 14		**34.75**
Total Due			**34.75**
Late Charge Reminder	A late charge may apply on Dec 16 if your payment has not been received, however, your bill must still be paid before the DUE BY date to avoid any other penalties. (See Reverse)		
Whom to call	For billing questions call:		
	Pacific Bell	No Charge	811-7000
	AT&T	No Charge	1 800 222-0300
	When moving or placing an order call:		
	Pacific Bell	No Charge	811-7200
	The NEW 811 NUMBERS may not be available in your area. Call the Business office number on your bill or call Directory Assistance for an alternate number.		

1. How much is this telephone bill?
2. When does the person need to pay?
3. How much was the last bill?
4. What numbers do you call if you want to ask a question about the bill?
5. If you are moving, what number do you need to call?

PART 4	# Writing

Using the Simple Present Tense

1 Read this letter to a pen pal. (Pen pals are persons who write to each other but may never have met.) The letter is from a real student from Los Angeles.

> Dear Pen Pal,
>
>   My name is María González. I am 20 years old. I live in Los Angeles, California. I live with my friends from Mexico. I work in a clothing factory, decorating clothes. For example, I sew jewelry on fancy dresses. Sometimes movie stars wear them.
>
>   I like to listen to Mexican banda music. Banda music is like a cross between American country music and rock and roll, but the bands sing in Spanish. I like to read, and I enjoy ice skating. In Los Angeles, you have to go ice skating at indoor skating rinks, because it never gets cold enough outside for ice. It's fun to go ice skating when it's 90 degrees outside.
>
>   My favorite TV programs are the National Geographic specials. I like them because I am very interested in foreign countries. I would like to travel to China and France some day.
>
>   Sincerely yours,
>   María González

Write three interesting things about María.

Example

María is from Mexico.

1. _____

2. _____

3. _____

In Chapter 2 you practiced the simple past tense and the *going-to* future tense. The simple present tense is used to talk about things that are true without referring to the past or the future. For example, María's sentences in her letter are mostly in the simple present. When you wrote about María in the previous activity, you used verbs in the third-person singular form.

Third-Person Singular Endings

We often use the simple present tense when we talk about our everyday lives.

    I go to school four days a week.

Remember, if the subject is third person singular (*he, she,* or *it*), we ad *-s* or *-es* to the verb.

    My brother works every day.
    He goes to school at night.

---

2   Look at the reading "Our Family Reunion" on page 40. Underline the verbs in the simple present tense. Circle the verbs with *-s* or *-es* endings.

Practicing the Writing Process

3   **Exploring Ideas: Using Personal Information.** Write information about yourself in the blanks. Use María's letter to help you.

1. My name is _____.

2. I am _____ years old.

3. I live _____.

4. On weekends I like to _____.

5. I like _____. (music, movies, etc.)

6. _____.

7. _____.

8. _____.

Now interview a classmate. First write down the questions to ask. Then fill in the blanks with your classmate's answers.

1. _What's your name_ _____?

   _____ 's name is _____.

2. _____?

   _____ is _____ years old.

3. _____?

   _____.

4. _____ on weekends?

   _____.

5. _____?

   _____ likes _____.

6. _____.

7. _____.

8. _____.

4   **Writing the First Draft.**   Write a pen-pal letter to María. Or perhaps your teacher will help you find a real pen pal in another country. This can be done on the Internet. You can send your letter by e-mail.

Dear _____

_____

_____

_____

_____

_____

_____

_____

                                      _____

                                      _____

5   **Editing.**   When you write about something, be very specific and add details (extra or special information). That way your writing will be more interesting.

General (not interesting):
   I like music.

Specific (more interesting):
   I like classic rock and roll from the sixties, especially the Rolling Stones and the Beatles. I have a hundred CDs.

General (not interesting):
   I live in Tokyo.

Specific (more interesting):
   I live in Tokyo, the capital city of Japan. There are 12 million people in Tokyo.

Another way to be specific is to include details by adding a second sentence beginning with "For example."

   I like to run. For example, last month I ran in a 14-mile marathon.

Rewrite these sentences and make them more interesting and specific. You can use your own information or your imagination.

Example

   I like movies.

   I like science fiction movies. For example, my favorite movie is *Star Wars Episode I: The Phantom Menace.*

1. I like movies.

   _____

   _____

2. I like music.

   _____

   _____

3. I like sports.

   _____

   _____

Now look back at Exercise 1. Exploring Ideas: Using Personal Information. Can you make your answers for Nos. 3, 4, and 5 more interesting? Try to add details, for example.

3. I live _____.

4. On weekends I like to _____.

5. I like _____. (music, movies, etc.)

Next check your pen-pal letter. Use this checklist to correct any mistakes.

Editing Checklist

Are sentences in the simple present talking about an action in general?

Are the simple present verbs in the simple form (*go, watch, play, shop*)?

Do the third-person singular verb forms end in *-s* or *-es?*

Are there good details? (I like rap music, especially Dr. Dre.)

Do your sentences begin with capital letters?

Do other words in your writing need capital letters?

Show your writing to another student. Can you think of more details? Ask your classmate questions.

6   **Writing the Second Draft.**   Now you are ready to write your second draft. When you have finished, give it to your teacher.

Writing a Journal

Write a journal entry about your everyday activities. Use the simple present tense.

I get up early every day. I take the bus to school. I have classes until two o'clock. Then I go home for a big lunch.

Video Activities: Pet Behavior

Before You Watch.

1. Which of these animals are common pets?

    a. dog   b. lion   c. cat   d. chicken

2. What is an animal shelter for?

    a. sick pets   b. bad pets   c. homeless pets

Watch.

1. What was the dog owner's problem?

    a. The dogs ate a lot.

    b. The dogs were noisy.

    c. The dogs destroyed things.

2. What was the dogs' problem?

    a. They were bored.   b. They were afraid.   c. They were hungry.

3. What is Emily's business?

    a. She adopts dogs.   b. She teaches dogs.   c. She visits dogs.

4. What do most dogs need?

    a. other dogs   b. a lot of toys   c. people's attention

5. Everyone who adopts a dog from the animal shelter promises to

    a. spend time with the dog.

    b. send the dog to school.

    c. hire Emily.

Watch Again.

1. What are the dogs' names?

    _____ Weiner   _____ Arnold

    _____ Max   _____ Taylor

    _____ Otis

2. Check the things that the dogs damaged.

    _____ couch   _____ fireplace

    _____ coffee table   _____ curtains

    _____ bed   _____ chair

    _____ carpet   _____ table

After You Watch.   Write a paragraph about a pet. If you do not have a pet, use your imagination. Include this information. What kind of pet do you have? What is your pet's name? How often does your pet cause trouble? What does your pet do? How often do you play with your pet?

Chapter 4

Health Care

IN THIS CHAPTER

You will read about sleep and health. You will also take a test to answer this question: are *you* healthy? You are also going to write an opinion paragraph.

| PART 1 | # Sleep and Health |

Before You Read

1   **Vocabulary Preview.**   Sometimes we can make an adjective from a noun by adding a *y* to the singular form of the noun. For example, to change the noun *rain* into an adjective, we add a *y—rainy*—this means "there's a lot of rain." Complete the following sentences with the appropriate adjective.

1.   If something has a lot of dirt, it's _dirty_____.

2.   If you have a lot of <u>luck</u>, you are _____.

3.   If there's a lot of <u>wind</u>, it's _____.

4.   If there are a lot of <u>rocks</u> on the beach, it is _____.

5.   If you need a lot of <u>sleep</u>, you are _____.

2   **Making Good Guesses.**   Remember that sometimes you can understand new words without a dictionary. For example, you can figure out or guess the meaning from other words in the sentence. Guess the meaning of the underlined words. Circle the letter to complete the sentence.

1.   People who are <u>sleep-deprived</u> are always tired, often get angry easily, and don't do as well as other people on tests.

     Sleep-deprived most likely means _____.

     a.   having a lot of sleep

     b.   getting angry easily

     c.   not having enough sleep

2.   He fell asleep and died in a terrible car <u>crash</u>.

     Crash most likely means _____.

     a.   a long trip

     b.   an accident

     c.   a small problem

3.   George liked <u>mental</u> work, but not physical work. He liked to do math problems, but he hated to work in the garden.

     Mental most likely means _____.

     a.   in your mind

     b.   with your body

     c.   paying a lot of money

4. Last week we worked 30 hours. This week the company <u>increased</u> our work hours to 40.

   Increased most likely means _____.

   a. make something smaller

   b. stop doing something

   c. make something larger

5. He started working when he was ten. He worked hard all his life. He is <u>used to</u> hard work. "I like hard work," he says.

   When you are *used to* something, most likely you _____.

   a. know a lot about it and it is familiar

   b. don't know anything about it and it is new

   c. know something about it but you don't like it

6. When a government spends more money than it receives, it has a <u>deficit</u>. The government must try to eliminate the deficit.

   The word *deficit* most likely means _____.

   a. taxes

   b. money from a government

   c. spending without enough money

Read

3 Read the article. Don't use your dictionary. If you don't know some words, try to guess their meaning.

Sleep and Health

[A] One of the easiest and cheapest ways to help your health is just to sleep eight hours or more every night, but more and more people in the world are not sleeping enough. According to the World Health Organization, over half the people in the world may be sleep-deprived. The result of this is not just a lot of tired people; in the United States alone, sleepy drivers cause at least 100,000 car crashes and 1500 deaths a year. Problems with sleep can also cause mental problems, as well as medical problems such as high blood pressure, diabetes, thyroid problems, and heart problems.

[B] "Anything that slows down work is a waste," said Thomas Edison, the inventor of the light bulb. After the invention of the light bulb, he predicted that work days could be increased to 24 hours a day. American culture values work and often doesn't value sleep; in fact, people who sleep a lot are often called "lazy." Many famous business and political leaders say proudly, "I only have time to sleep four or five hours a night." Students, especially college students, often sleep only a few hours a night. They often say, "I'm used to sleeping only a little."

[C]   But, according to experts, sleep is like money. If you sleep only five hours a day, you don't "get used to it," but instead, build up a "sleep deficit." "It's like a credit card," says Dr. James Maas, the author of *Power Sleep*. "You are only borrowing time. You always have to pay it back." The more hours you don't sleep, the more hours you should sleep to "pay back" the hours on your "sleep credit card." For example, if you sleep four hours on Monday and then sleep eight hours on Tuesday, on Wednesday you will still have a "sleep deficit" of four hours. This deficit can continue for months or even years. People with a "sleep deficit" are sleep-deprived; driving and making decisions can be dangerous for these people.

[D]   Stanley Coren's research showed that when people sleep ten hours, they do better on tests of mental ability and mood. Research also shows that when people sleep in special rooms without clocks or windows, they usually sleep nine or ten hours. This probably means most people should sleep nine or ten hours every night. If this is true, even more than half the people in the world may be running a "sleep deficit." You didn't do your homework last night? Maybe you can tell your teacher that you were working hard on your sleep deficit.

[E]   Winston Churchill, the famous leader of England during World War II, worked late at night, but he also often took naps (short sleeps) during the day. He knew sleep was important. He once said, "Don't think you will be doing less work because you sleep during the day. That's a foolish idea held by people who have no imagination. You will be able to do more."

After You Read

4   **Finding the Main Ideas.**   Circle the letter of the main idea of "Sleep and Health."

a.   Sleepy drivers are dangerous.

b.   Students should do their homework.

c.   Getting enough sleep is very important.

d.   Anything that slows down work is a waste.

Cross-Cultural Note

In English we say "time is money." When we talk about time and money, we often use the same verbs. For example, we "spend" time, and we "spend" money. We "waste" time, and we "waste" money. We "save" time, and we "save" money. Does your language have this pattern? In your culture do people talk about time and money with the same words?

Read the article again. Match the following main ideas with the correct paragraphs. Write the letter (A, B, C, D, or E) of each paragraph in the appropriate blank.

___B___   American culture values working more than sleeping.

_____   Sleep deprivation is a big problem.

_____   This paragraph really says "good-bye" to the reader.

_____   People may need 9 or 10 hours of sleep.

_____   When you don't sleep enough, you need to sleep more later.

Discussing the Reading

5 Discuss the following questions in small groups.

1. How many hours do you sleep every night?
2. Do you ever feel tired?
3. In your culture do people work more and sleep less?

PART 2 # Are You Healthy?

Before You Read

1 Before you take the following test, answer this question: how is your health? (good, average, or bad?)

a.

b.

c.

d.

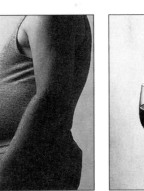

e.

f.

Read

2 Everyone wants to be healthy. Take the test. It will answer the question "Am I healthy?" Circle the letters of your answers.

1. Do you eat foods with sugar such as candy, donuts, and ice cream?

   a. never   b. sometimes   c. often

2. Do you eat a *good* breakfast every day, not just coffee and a doughnut?

   a. yes   b. usually   c. no

3. Do you eat fruits and vegetables every day?

   a. 5 or more   b. 1 or 2   c. no

4. Do you smoke?

   a. never

   b. 1–10 cigarettes every day

   c. 10+ cigarettes every day

5. Do you drink coffee or cola?

   a. no

   b. 1–2 cups or glasses every day

   c. 3–10 cups or glasses every day

6. Do you sleep 7–8 hours every night?

   a. yes   b. no

7. Are you overweight?

   a. no   b. 5–19 pounds   c. 20–50 pounds

8. How far do you walk every day?

   a. 1–5 miles   b. 1/2–1 mile   c. 0 miles

9. How often do you eat eggs?

   a. seldom or never   b. 2–3 times every week   c. every day

10. Do you exercise (run, swim, play a team sport)?

    a. often   b. 1 time every week   c. seldom or never

11. How much alcohol do you drink every week?

    a. 0–7 glasses   b. 8–15 glasses   c. 16+ glasses

12. Do you worry, or are you unhappy?

    a. seldom   b. sometimes   c. often

Cross-Cultural Note

In some countries, people are trying to stop smoking. In other countries, more people (especially young people) are beginning to smoke. What is the situation in your home country?

How healthy are you?

Every answer a = 3.

Every answer b = 2.

Every answer c = 0.

YOUR SCORE: _____

30–36 = You're probably very healthy.

25–29 = You might need to make some changes.

0–24 = You might not be healthy.

After You Read

Discussing the Reading

3 Work with a partner. Look at your answers and your partner's answers to the questions on the health test. Give your partner advice. Use *should* and *shouldn't*.

Example

You should eat a good breakfast.

Dictionary Use—Guide Words

Sometimes you can't understand a new word without a dictionary. If you want to find a word fast, you need to use guide words. Guide words are at the top of every dictionary page, usually in the left and right corners.

Example

Here is a dictionary page. The guide words are *picnic* and *pig*.

The first word on this page is *picnic*. The last word is *pig*. The words on a dictionary page come between these two guide words. You just need to look at the guide words, and you'll know if your new word is on this page.

picnic	386	pig

picnic (4) [pik'nik], *n.* a meal planned for eating outdoors. **Ex.** *They ate their picnic beside the river.* —*v.* have a picnic. **Ex.** *We picnicked in the woods.* —**pic'nick·er,** *n.* **Ex.** *After lunch, the picnickers made up teams for a game of baseball.*

picture (1) [pik'čər], *n.* 1. a painting, drawing, or photograph. **Ex.** *That picture of the President is seen often in the newspaper.* 2. that which strongly resembles another; an image. **Ex.** *She is the picture of her mother.* 3. a description. **Ex.** *The author gives a lively picture of his life as a sailor.* 4. a motion picture; movie. **Ex.** *The whole family enjoyed the picture we saw last night.* —*v.* describe. **Ex.** *The speaker pictured the scene in colorful words.* —**pic·tor'i·al,** *adj.*

pie (2) [pay'], *n.* a baked dish consisting of a thin shell, and sometimes a cover, made of flour and cooking oil and filled with fruit, meat, etc. **Ex.** *She put the pie in the oven to bake.*

piece (1) [piys'], *n.* 1. an amount or a part considered as an individual unit. **Ex.** *Please give me a piece of writing paper.* 2. a part taken away from something larger. **Ex.** *She cut the pie into six pieces.* 3. a coin. **Ex.** *Can you change this fifty-cent piece?* —*v.* join together; make whole. **Ex.** *She pieced together the broken dish.* —**go to pieces,** become upset or excited. **Ex.** *He goes to pieces when I disagree with him.*

piecemeal [piys'miyl'], *adv.* one part at a time; piece by piece. **Ex.** *He put the machine together piecemeal in his spare time.*

piecework [piys'wərk'], *n.* work paid for by the piece finished instead of by the hour, day, etc. **Ex.** *She does piecework at home.*

pier (3) [pi:r'], *n.* a structure built over the water and used as a landing place for ships and boats. **Ex.** *The ship is at pier seven.*

pierce (4) [pirs'], *v.* 1. break into or through. **Ex.** *The knife had pierced the wall.* 2. make a hole or opening in. **Ex.** *Many girls have their ears pierced for earrings.* 3. force a way through. **Ex.** *They tried to pierce the enemy's defense.* 4. deeply or sharply affect the senses or feelings. **Ex.** *They were pierced by the icy winds.*

pig (2) [pig'], *n.* a farm animal with a broad nose and fat body, raised for its meat.

PIG

4   Use your dictionary. Find the following pages quickly. What are the guide words? Write them on the blanks. If there are no guide words, write the first and last words.

1. page 32   _____   _____

2. page 196   _____   _____

3. page 15   _____   _____

4. page 203   _____   _____

5. page 78   _____   _____

5   Can you find the words on the left on dictionary pages with the guide words on the right? Write *yes* or *no* on each line.

			Guide Words
1.	_no_	swim	sleep—smoke
2.	____	fact	face—fan
3.	____	nice	never—night
4.	____	long	learn—listen
5.	____	overweight	old—pitcher
6.	____	grow	gray—health
7.	____	store	still—sugar
8.	____	young	vegetable—walk

6   Now use your dictionary to find the following words. Use the guide words in the dictionary for help. Write the page number for each word.

Word	Page	Word	Page	Word	Page
interesting	_____	message	_____	noise	_____
meditate	_____	attack	_____	serious	_____
noise	_____	emergency	_____	heart	_____

7   **Building Vocabulary.**   Cross out the word that does not belong in each group.

1. brother   ~~friend~~   cousin   sister

2. fruits   meat   vegetables   glass

3. robot   microchip   computer   fruit

4. expert   scientist   salesperson   researcher

5. borrow   lend   health   deficit

6. think   walk   learn   remember

7. sleepy   nap   student   sleep

8. difficult   unhappy   terrible   begin

9. nuclear   single-parent   unhappy   traditional

PART 3	# Being Sick

George is sick. He's in the hospital. Here is a card from his friends at work. Many people write little messages when they sign a card. Sign your name on the card and write one of the following messages to George. (Or use your imagination and write your own message.)

　　Get well soon, George.

　　We miss you.

　　Hope to see you soon.

a.

b.

The words in Column A are from the get-well card. On the lines, write the letters of the words from Column B that match the meaning of the words in Column A.

A		B	
1. _b_ "dear to us"		a.	George
2. ____ "as good as new"		b.	we like you very much
3. ____ "a special someone"		c.	okay again, healthy again
4. ____ "you're better"		d.	in a short time
5. ____ "soon"		e.	you're healthy

George has a lot of health problems. Here are some of the medicines he must take every day. Read the directions for each medicine.

    a. Take two tablets in the morning. TAKE WITH FOOD

    b. Take one capsule after every meal.

    c. Take one teaspoonful before bed. DO NOT TAKE WITH FOOD

   d. Take two tablespoonfuls four times a day.

Match the types of medicine with the times George must take the medicine. Write the letters of the pictures on the lines.

1. __b__ He ate lunch.

2. _____ He is eating breakfast.

3. _____ He is at work.

4. _____ He is going to sleep.

Using the information from the previous exercise, complete the directions for George.

1. _George must take two tablets with food in the morning._

2. _____

3. _____

4. _____

PART 4

Writing

Using Sentence Patterns

Sentence Pattern 5.   Read the information and examine the sentence patterns in the box. Then do the exercise that follows.

subject	+	modal	+	simple form of verb
He		should		study.
I		will		work.
People		are going to		complain.
You		have to		go.

The modals add the opinion of the speaker or writer. *Should* adds "I think it is a good idea or the correct thing to do." *Will* adds "I believe it is definitely going to happen in the future." *Be going to* adds "this action is in the future." *Have to* adds "This action is necessary or required."

The article "Sleep and Health" uses the modal *should* three times. Write all three sentences on the following lines.

1. _____

2. _____

3. _____

We often use the modal *should* to give advice. Write one piece of advice about each of the following ideas. Remember to use the simple form of the verb.

Example

   To be healthy _you should exercise._

1. To have money _____

2. To have friends _____

3. To learn English _____

4. To be happy _____

Now work with your classmates. Read aloud your pieces of advice from the previous exercise. Write down two other pieces of advice for each topic.

1. To have money _____

   _____

2. To have friends _____

   _____

3. To learn English _____

   _____

4. To be happy _____

   _____

Here is a student's answer to the question "Should education be free in this country?" It is a simple opinion paragraph. Read the paragraph and the information that follows. Then do the exercise.

   Education should be free in this country for several good reasons. First, it is the fair thing to do. All people should have a chance for an education. Second, education is good for the country. A country is strong if everyone has a good education. Third, free education helps people's health. When people have a good education, they will exercise, stop smoking, and eat more healthy foods. For these reasons, education should be free in this country.

A typical outline for paragraphs in academic writing is the following:

1. Topic Sentence: statement of opinion

   a. reason number 1 + explanation (supporting statement)

   b. reason number 2 + explanation (supporting statement)

   c. reason number 3 + explanation (supporting statement)

2. Conclusion: summary

Look at the opinion paragraph again. There are eight sentences. Match the sentences to the following outline. Write each sentence in the appropriate blank.

1. Topic Sentence: statement of opinion

   <u>Education should be free in this country for several good reasons.</u>

   a. reason number 1

   _____

   + explanation (supporting statement)

   _____

   b. reason number 2

   _____

   + explanation (supporting statement)

   _____

   c. reason number 3

   _____

   + explanation (supporting statement)

   _____

2. Conclusion: summary

   _____

Practicing the Writing Process

1 **Exploring Ideas: Brainstorming and Free Writing.** You are going to write an opinion paragraph that answers this question: should tobacco be illegal (against the law) in your country? Sometimes you can get ideas by brainstorming on your own, for example, when you freewrite. Other times it's good to work with a group or the whole class and get ideas together. In a group or as a class, make a list of reasons tobacco should be made illegal and reasons tobacco shouldn't be made illegal. On separate paper, write down ideas for both sides of the argument.

    Now decide which side you are on. Think about your argument and freewrite your ideas. Work with a partner. Read aloud your ideas. Then discuss them with your partner.

2 **Writing the First Draft.** Write a first draft of your paragraph. Begin with "This country should make tobacco illegal" or "This country shouldn't make tobacco illegal." When necessary, use modals from the list on page 63.

3   **Editing.**   Check your opinion paragraph. Use the following checklist to correct any mistakes.

Editing Checklist

Are the verbs used with modals in the simple form (*study, work, discover, go*)?

Are the modals correct (*should* if you think something is a good idea or the correct thing to do, *will* if you believe something is definitely going to happen in the future, etc.)?

Do your sentences begin with capital letters?

Do other words in the writing need capital letters?

Do your sentences end with periods?

Show your paragraph to another student. Read each other's paragraphs. Does your partner's paragraph have a topic sentence, interesting reasons and explanations, a conclusion? Use the Editing Checklist to check your classmate's paragraph.

4   **Writing the Second Draft.**   Write your second draft and give it to your teacher.

Video Activities: Brain Surgery

Before You Watch.

1. When a doctor has to fix a heart, what does he or she do?

    a. an examination   b. a transplant   c. surgery

2. What part of your body controls movement?

    a. your eyes   b. your heart   c. your brain   d. your leg

Watch.

1. What is this a picture of?

    a. a brain

    b. a heart

    c. a hand

2. Check the ways that Dr. Francel's surgery is different from others.

    _____ It's faster.   _____ He uses computers.

    _____ It's cheaper.   _____ He operates on brains.

3. Before the surgery, Mr. Previt's hand _____.

    a. hurts   b. cannot move   c. shakes

4. During the surgery, Mr. Previt is _____.

    a. sleeping   b. awake   c. shaking

5. After the surgery, Mr. Previt _____.

    a. can hold a glass   b. cannot feel his hand   c. can talk better

Watch Again.   Complete the sentences with numbers from the box.

| 1 1/2 to 2 | 12 | 100 | 2 |

1. Dr. Francel does this surgery in _____ hours.

2. Other doctors do this surgery in _____ hours.

3. Dr. Francel can operate on _____ patients in a day.

4. A human hair is about _____ microns thick.

After You Watch.   This paragraph has seven errors. Find the errors and rewrite the paragraph correctly.

Many doctors performing brain surgery but Dr. Francel use a new method. He operate with a computer. He can to work very quickly with the computer. He can also is very accurate. All doctors should to use these computers. Computers would to make surgery cheaper, faster, and better.

Chapter 5

Men and Women

IN THIS CHAPTER

You will read about differences in men's and women's style of conversation. Also, you will find the answers to these questions: What do men say about women? What do women say about men? And you will learn to write a story (a narrative).

<table>
<tr><td>**PART 1**</td></tr>
</table>

Men's Talk and Women's Talk in the United States

Before You Read

1 Look at the pictures and read what the people say. Then answer and discuss the following questions with a partner or group.

1. In picture 1, the man doesn't understand something. What is it?
2. In picture 1, the woman is a little angry. Why?
3. In picture 2, the woman is unhappy. Why?
4. In picture 2, the man is unhappy. Why?
5. Do men and women talk in different ways?

Picture 1

Picture 2

2   **Vocabulary Preview.**   Sometimes you can understand a new word because the meaning is after the phrase "in other words."

Example

The scientist had a good <u>imagination</u>; in other words, he thought of new, creative ideas easily.

You use your imagination to <u>think up new, creative ideas.</u>

Write the definition (meaning) of the following underlined words. Look for the meaning after the phrase "in other words."

1.   My twin brothers are very <u>similar</u>. In other words, they like the same things and play in the same way. They aren't very different.

    Similar means not _____

2.   Boys <u>brag</u>; in other words, they say good things about themselves.

    When people brag, they say _____

3.   Little boys are usually <u>active</u>; in other words, they do things.

    Active people don't sit and do nothing. They _____

We can often guess the meaning of a word from the words around it—the context. Use the context of the following sentences to understand the five words in the exercise that follows. Then match the words with the definitions. Do not use your dictionary.

1. I apologized to my wife. I said, "I'm really sorry about last night."

2. My boss gives me orders all the time. He says, "copy this," or "get the mail," or "make coffee." I don't like it.

3. He has a high position in the company. Everyone thinks he will be president some day.

4. I have a good suggestion: I think we should have some lunch now.

5. We are equal in the company. We have exactly the same position.

1. __b__ apologize   a. ideas ("Maybe we should do this.")

2. _____ orders   b. to say "I'm sorry"

3. _____ position   c. commands ("Do this.")

4. _____ suggestions   d. same

5. _____ equal   e. place in a group ("president")

Read

3   Read the following article. Don't use a dictionary. Instead use the diagrams, examples, and words in parentheses to understand new words. Also remember you can find the meaning of a new word after the phrase "in other words."

Men's Talk and Women's Talk in the United States

[A] Marriage is often not easy. Love often is not easy. Sometimes friendship between a man and a woman is not easy. Maybe a man and a woman love or like each other, but they argue. They get angry. Later they apologize, but it happens again and again. What's the problem? Are men and women really very different?

[B]   Deborah Tannen says yes. Men and women are very different. Tannen teaches at Georgetown University. She writes books about the ways people talk. She believes that men and women talk—and think—in different ways. She tells about some differences in her book *You Just Don't Understand.*

[C]   The differences, Tannen says, begin when men and women are children. Very young boys and girls are similar to each other. In other words, they like the same things and play in the same ways. They aren't very different. But then there is a change.

[D]   When children in the United States are five or six years old, boys usually play in large groups. One boy gives orders. For example, he says, "Take this," "Go over there," and "Be on this team." He is the leader. Boys also brag. In other words, they say good things about themselves. They do this to have a high position. Position in the group is important to boys.

high position

low position

[E]   Girls in the United States usually play in small groups or with one other girl. A girl's "best friend"—her very, very good friend—is important to her. Girls don't often give orders; they give suggestions. For example, they say, "Let's go over there," "Maybe we should do this," and "Do you want to play with that?" Girls don't usually have a leader, and they don't often brag. Everyone has an equal position.

equal positions

[F]   Little boys are usually active; they do things. Much of the time, little girls sit together and talk. When children grow up, nothing really changes. Men usually do things together. Or they talk about activities such as sports and things such as cars and world problems. They talk to give or get information. But for women, people and feelings are important. Women often talk to show interest and love. Although a man and a woman speak the same language, sometimes they don't understand each other. Men's talk and women's talk are almost two different languages. But maybe men and women can learn to understand each other if they understand the differences in speech.

After You Read

4 **Finding the Main Ideas.**   Which sentences from the article are about men? Which sentences are about women? Write M (men) or W (women) on each line.

1.   _M_   When they are children, they usually play in large groups.

2.   _____   When they are children, they usually play in small groups or with one friend.

3.   _____   There usually isn't a leader in the children's play group.

4.   _____   One child in the play group is the leader.

5.   _____   They talk to show interest and love.

6.   _____   They talk to give or get information.

5 Remember a synopsis gives the information of a text in a very short way. Here are three synopses of the article you just read. None of them is wrong—they all have information from the article. But remember, the best synopsis needs to give <u>all</u> the important information. Choose the best one, then compare your answer with a partner's.

A. Marriage is not easy. Men and women may argue. They may apologize later. This problem can happen many times. Men and women can learn to understand each other if they listen to each other.

B. Men and women talk and think differently. These differences begin as children. Men often talk to give or get information. Women often talk to show interest and love. These differences can cause problems.

C. Deborah Tannen teaches at Georgetown University. She is a writer. She writes about how people talk. She says that men and women are different. She wrote a book called *You Just Don't Understand.*

Discussing the Reading

6 Talk with a small group about your answers to the following questions.

1. When you were a child, did you play in a big group or a small group? Did you have a best friend?

2. Would you like to have a high position in a group, or would you like to be in a group with equal positions?

3. What do you sometimes argue about with your husband? Wife? Boyfriend? Girlfriend?

4. In your country, do men and women talk differently? If so, give examples.

Cross-Cultural Note

The article is about men and women in the United States. In your home country, do men and women talk in different ways? For example, do men talk to women the same way as men talk to other men? Do women talk to other women differently than they talk to men? Do they act differently? Do they work at different jobs?

| **PART 2** | # He Said/She Said: A U.S. Couple |

Before You Read

1 **Making Predictions.** Look at the pictures. Where are the man and woman? Whom are they talking to? Why? Discuss your answers with a partner or group.

Read

2 Listen to the following article, then read it quickly.

He Said/She Said: A U.S. Couple

[A] Well, Doctor, I'm beginning to worry about my marriage. My wife and I just don't understand each other. She doesn't like to do things with me. She won't play tennis or baseball with me. She doesn't like to fix the car with me. She doesn't work on the house with me—you know, paint the house or fix the roof. She doesn't listen when I talk about interesting things: sports, money, or world politics. Sometimes she gets angry with me about unimportant things. And she talks and talks and talks about uninteresting things. What's wrong with her?

Cross-Cultural Note

Sometimes American couples go to a marriage counselor for help with their marriage. Does this happen in your culture? If not, what do people do about marriage problems?

[B] Well, Doctor, I'm beginning to worry about my marriage. My husband and I just don't understand each other. We both work full-time, but I do all the work at home—you know, fix dinner, wash clothes, and clean the house. His life is easy; he has only one job. I have two! Sometimes I feel so lonely. When he's home, he reads the newspaper or watches TV. He doesn't talk with me; he talks at me. He only talks with his friends. He doesn't listen if I tell him about my day. He isn't interested in our friends and relatives. Sometimes he gives me orders. Sometimes he tells me about sports or politics, but I don't like it because I feel like a student in school. What's wrong with him?

After You Read

3 Read the article again. Then do the exercise.

The man in the article is unhappy about many things. What does he say? Put checks on the appropriate lines.

1. ____✔____ His wife doesn't like to do things with him.

2. _____ His wife talks about uninteresting things.

3. _____ His wife gives him orders.

4. _____ His wife doesn't listen when he talks about sports, money, or politics.

The woman is also unhappy about many things. What does she say? Put checks on the lines.

5. _____ Her husband gets angry about unimportant things.

6. _____ She goes to work and does all the work at home too.

7. _____ Her husband doesn't talk with her.

8. _____ Her husband gives her orders.

4 Students usually need to read fast because they have to read many books each year. Also, they can understand more if they read fast. Look at the example. Then do the exercise.

Example

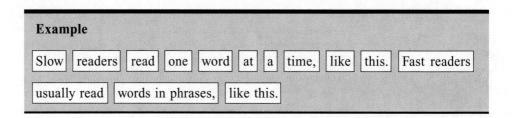

Slow | readers | read | one | word | at | a | time, | like | this. | Fast readers | usually read | words in phrases, | like this.

Read the following sentences in phrases. Read silently; in other words, do not speak.

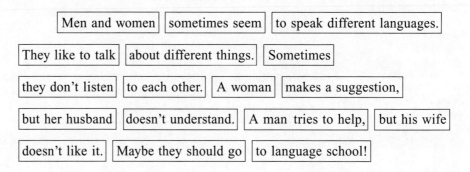

Men and women | sometimes seem | to speak different languages. They like to talk | about different things. | Sometimes they don't listen | to each other. | A woman | makes a suggestion, but her husband | doesn't understand. | A man tries to help, | but his wife doesn't like it. | Maybe they should go | to language school!

Now read the paragraph. Focus on the phrases, not the separate words:

   Men and women sometimes seem to speak different languages. They like to talk about different things. Sometimes they don't listen to each other. A woman makes a suggestion, but her husband doesn't understand. A man tries to help, but his wife doesn't like it. Maybe they should go to language school!

---

5   **Building Vocabulary.**   Complete the following sentences. Circle the letters of the answers. There is one answer for each blank.

1. Their _____ are very important to them.

   a. leader   c. cultural

   b. friends   d. friendship

2. Could you please give me some _____?

   a. information   c. active

   b. important   d. suggestion

3. Maybe we should _____.

   a. advice   c. show

   b. happen   d. apologize

4. That information is _____.

   a. brag   c. orders

   b. wrong   d. argue

Are the meanings of the following words similar or different? Write S (similar) or D (different) on the lines.

1. __S__ sleepy—tired   4. _____ waste—deficit

2. _____ suggestions—activities   5. _____ apologize—brag

3. _____ family—relatives   6. _____ leader—position

Discussing the Reading

6   In small groups, talk about your answers to the following questions.

1. Are people in your country similar to or different from the man and woman pictured on page 75?

2. If you're a woman, what do you talk about with other women? What do you talk about with men? If you're a man, what do you talk about with other men? What do you talk about with women?

PART 3   Wedding Customs

1   Look at the wedding invitation. There is also an invitation to the reception (the reception is the party after the wedding) and a response card. People use the response card to tell the family that they will come or they won't come.

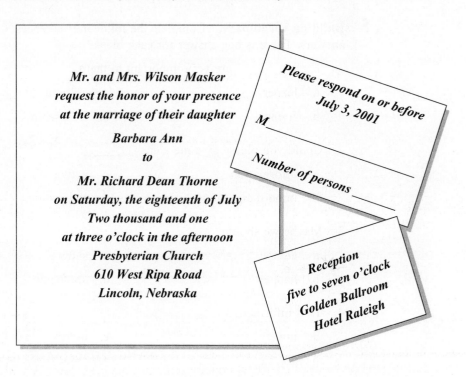

Now complete the following sentences about the invitation. Circle the letters of the correct endings.

1.   The time of the wedding is _____.

a.   3:10 P.M.   b.   3:00 A.M.   c.   3:00 P.M.

2.   The date of the wedding is _____.

a.   July 3, 2001   b.   July 18, 2001   c.   July 8, 2001

3.   The groom (the man getting married) is _____.

a.   Wilson Masker   b.   Richard Dean Thorne   c.   Barbara Ann

4.   The last name of the bride (the woman getting married) is _____.

a.   Ann   b.   Masker   c.   Thorne

5.   You should answer the invitation _____.

a.   before July 18   b.   after July 3   c.   by July 3

2 Richard and Barbara got many wedding presents. Write the names of the gifts in the box by the pictures.

a blanket	a toaster	a coffee maker
a teapot	a flower vase	a microwave oven

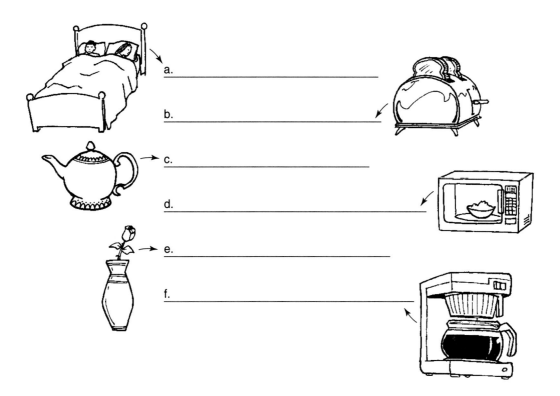

a. _____

b. _____

c. _____

d. _____

e. _____

f. _____

3 In the United States, when you get a gift or present, it is polite to write a thank-you note. People usually write about how they will use the gift. How will people use the following presents? Draw lines to match the gifts and their uses.

1. blanket   a. to make coffee every day

2. coffee maker   b. to keep warm all winter

3. toaster   c. to serve tea to our special guests

4. teapot   d. to show our flowers

5. flower vase   e. to make toast every morning

4   Complete the thank-you notes below.

a.

Dear Mr. and Mrs. Sanchez,
    Thank you for the beautiful toaster. We
will use it _____ _____ _____ .

_____ _____ _____

    Thanks again.

                    Sincerely,

                    _____

b.

Dear Mrs. Sprunk,
    Thank you for the _____
teapot. We _____ use it _____
_____ _____ _____ our

_____ _____ .

    Thanks _____ .

                    _____

                    _____

c.

Dear Mr. Maloof,
    Thank you _____ _____ _____
flower vase. We _____ _____ _____

_____ _____ .

    Thanks _____ .

                    _____

                    _____

d.

Mrs. Potter, _____ _____ _____

coffeemaker. _____ _____ .

_____ _____ _____

_____ _____ _____ _____

_____ _____ _____

_____ _____

PART 4

Writing

Using Sentence Patterns

Sentence Pattern 6.   Read the information and examine the sentence patterns. Then do the exercises that follow.

We learned that some verbs have an actor, an action, and a receiver of the action—*The car hit the tree.* These are called transitive verbs. We also learned that some verbs have only an actor and an action—*The man jumped.* These are called intransitive verbs. A few verbs describe an action that has an actor and two different receivers—often called the *direct object* and the *indirect object.*

subject	+	verb	+	indirect object (person)	+	direct object (thing)
I		told		Sally		the story.
John		gave		me		some money.
The teacher		asked		Kim		a question.
The waiter		brought		him		a soft drink.

Many of these verbs, for example, *bring*, can also be used with only a direct object or with both a direct object and an indirect object.

Example
He brought lunch.
He brought me lunch.

Use the following verbs in sentences. On the first blank, write a sentence with only a direct object. On the second blank, write a sentence with both a direct object and an indirect object. Make sure the indirect object comes <u>before</u> the direct object.

1. send: _____

    _____

2. pay: _____

    _____

3. sell: _____

    _____

4. ask: _____

_____

5. get: _____

_____

6. make: _____

_____

Sometimes students confuse the verbs *tell*, *say*, and *talk*. Look at the example. Then do the exercise.

Example

The teacher tells us stories.

The teacher says "Good morning" every day.

The teacher always talks to us before class.

Fill in the blanks with the past tense of *tell*, *say*, or *talk*.

1. John _____ Mary the answer.

2. I _____ "good-bye" to Mary.

3. Mary _____ to the teacher.

4. They _____ about sports all afternoon.

5. John _____, "I'm sorry."

6. Fred _____ me the story about the movie.

7. George _____ the teacher his problem.

8. _____ you _____ to the doctor yesterday?

Here is a picture story about Henry and Sadae. Look at each picture. Then look at the sentences in the box. In the blanks, write the correct sentences for each picture.

1

They met.

2

3
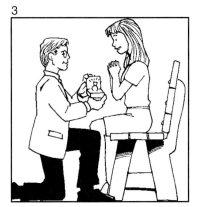

4

5

6

They were angry at each other.

They met.

He asked her to marry him.

They were in love.

They got married.

He never wanted to talk to her about work.

Practicing the Writing Process

A narrative is a story. It tells about a series of actions. Most often the simple past tense is used. Read the student's story about her parents meeting and marrying. Then follow the steps of the writing process.

My father met my mother in 1980. They met at a college dance. My father liked my mother right away, but my mother did not like my father. He asked her to go out on a date. She wanted to say no, but she was too polite and so she said yes. On their date they went to the movies and saw *Raging Bull*, a movie starring Robert De Niro. After the movie they talked for a long time; they even argued about the movie (he liked it but she didn't). My mother decided that my father was very intelligent. Then my mother started to become interested in him. Soon they were in love.

---

1 **Exploring Ideas: Free Writing.**   Write for ten minutes about how you met someone close to you; or tell about how your parents met. Don't worry about spelling or grammar.

Now tell a partner about your story. Don't read your freewrite aloud. Use your own words.

2 **Writing the First Draft.**   Write a first draft of your narrative.

3 **Editing.**   Now check your story. Here is a list of things to check for in your narrative.

Editing Checklist

Are the verbs you used transitive or intransitive?

Do any of the verbs have direct objects? Indirect objects? Both? Are these verbs used correctly?

Did you use the simple past tense? (Remember that most often the simple past tense is used in narratives.)

Do you have interesting details in your narrative?

Do your sentences begin with capital letters?

Do other words in the writing need capital letters?

Do your sentences end with periods or other final punctuation?

Make a group with three other students. Take turns and read your story to the others in your group.

4 **Writing the Second Draft.**   Write your second draft and give it to your teacher.

Chapter 6

Sleep and Dreams

IN THIS CHAPTER

You will read about sleep and dreams. You will read someone's dream narrative, and you will write about one of your dreams.

| PART 1 | # Sleep and Dreams |

Before You Read

1   Can you answer the following questions? Compare your answers with a partner or a group.

1. Why do we sleep?
2. Does everyone dream?
3. What do dreams mean?

You Try It!

Put a piece of paper and a pen or pencil next to your bed. When you wake up after a dream, write down as much as you can remember about it. You will need this information for Part 4.

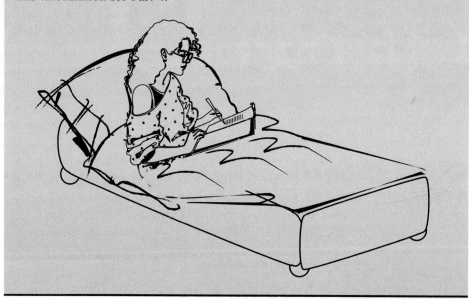

2   **Vocabulary Preview.**   Let's review some ways to understand the meaning of a word without using a dictionary. Write answers in the blanks.

Sometimes the meaning of a new word follows the word.

1. He says his theory is correct, but a theory is only an idea or a guess.

   A theory is   <u>an idea or a guess.</u>

The meaning of a word sometimes is in parentheses.

2. Our bodies produce a growth hormone (a chemical that helps us grow).

   A growth hormone is _____

Sometimes we can use our basic knowledge of the subject to guess the meaning.

3.   Scientists believe that birds evolved from dinosaurs.

Evolved means _____

The meaning of a word often follows a dash (—):

4.   The light turned on and off randomly—without any pattern or meaning.

Randomly means _____

Sometimes a writer uses two words that mean almost the same thing. If you know one word, you can guess the other.

5.   We need sleep to repair and fix our bodies.

Repair means something like _____

Other times we can use the context—the sentences that follow the word.

6.   There was a lot of evidence that George killed Mr. Smith. Police found George's gun in Mr. Smith's house. Also, two people saw George leaving Mr. Smith's house. In addition, everyone knew that George hated Mr. Smith.

Evidence is _____

7.   He was interested in Chinese culture. He studied Chinese art, history, language, and religion.

Some examples of culture are _____

8.   He wasted money all the time. He spent it on expensive meals, he bought new clothes he didn't need, and he drove an expensive car he couldn't afford.

Waste means _____

Are the following terms opposite or similar? Write O (for *opposite*) or S (for *similar*) on the line.

1.   _O_   activity—sleep
2.   _____   theory—idea
3.   _____   save—waste
4.   _____   lazy—active
5.   _____   disease—medical problem
6.   _____   megalopolis—city
7.   _____   company—business

Read

3 Read the article. Try to understand the meanings of new words without using a dictionary.

Sleep and Dreams

[A] No one really knows why we sleep. There are two theories, but a theory is only an idea or a guess—scientists don't know if these theories are correct or not.

[B]   One theory of sleep is called the "Repair Theory." This theory says that during the day we use many important chemicals in our bodies and brains. We need sleep to make new chemicals and repair and fix our bodies. One piece of evidence for this theory is that our bodies produce more of a growth hormone (a chemical that helps us grow) while we sleep.

[C]   Another theory is called the "Adaptive Theory." This theory says that sleep evolved because it stopped early humans and animals from wasting energy and putting themselves in danger from the other animals that killed and ate them; in other words, sleep kept them safe and out of trouble. It was necessary for their survival.

[D]   Whatever the reason for sleep, everyone sleeps and everyone dreams every night. Many times we don't remember our dreams, but we still dream. Like sleep, no one knows exactly why we dream or what dreams mean. There have been many theories about dreams throughout history. Many cultures believe that dreams can predict the future—that they can tell us what is going to happen to us. Sigmund Freud and other psychologists and psychiatrists believe that dreams can tell us about our feelings and desires.

[E]   However, some scientists now believe that dreams mean nothing at all—dreams are caused by the electrical activity in our brains while we sleep. These scientists believe that nerve cells fire randomly and our brains try to make a story out of these meaningless patterns. These scientists say that dreams seem crazy and without meaning sometimes because they are crazy and without any meaning at all.

After You Read

4 Read the article again. Every paragraph has a letter. What is the main idea of each paragraph? Write the paragraph letters on the lines.

____E____ Dreams may not mean anything.

_____ There are many theories about what dreams mean.

_____ Sleep may help our bodies prepare for a new day.

_____ Scientists have two theories about why we sleep.

_____ It is possible that sleep protected us from dangers.

Discussing the Reading

5   Talk about your answers to the following questions with a partner or a group.

1. Do you remember your dreams? What do you think dreams mean?

2. Does your family or culture have special meanings for some kinds of dreams? Do these dreams tell about the future?

3. Do you believe one of the two theories about why we sleep? Why or why not?

PART 2   # A Dream Narrative

Before You Read

1   Look at the picture. Discuss with a partner what is happening.

2   Circle the answer that is correct for you. Then share and discuss your answers with a partner or a group.

1.   How often do you remember your dreams?

   a.   Every night.

   b.   Often (four or five times a week).

   c.   Sometimes (once or twice a week).

   d.   Rarely (once a month).

   e.   Never.

2.   How often do you have nightmares (dreams that are scary or frightening)?

   a.   Every night.

   b.   Often (four or five times a week).

   c.   Sometimes (once or twice a week).

   d.   Rarely (once a month).

   e.   Never.

3.   How often do you understand your dreams?

   a.   Every time I dream.   d.   Rarely.

   b.   Often.   e.   Never.

   c.   Sometimes.

4.   Some people have a dream and they believe it tells about the future. Did this ever happen to you?

   a.   Many times.   c.   Once.

   b.   Several times.   d.   Never.

3   **Vocabulary Preview.**   Prefixes are syllables that come in front of the root of a word (the root is the "basic meaning" of the word). Prefixes change the meaning of the root word. For example, the prefix *un-* means "not" or "the opposite." So *unhappy* is the opposite of *happy*; *unhappy* means "not happy." Complete the following sentences.

1.   *Unfamiliar* means _____.

2.   *Uncomfortable* means _____.

3.   *Unmoving* means _____.

Note that sometimes the prefix *un-* does not change the meaning of the root word to its opposite. An example is the word *uneasy*. We don't say "the test was uneasy" because *uneasy* does not mean "not easy"; it means "not comfortable" and is usually used to talk about feelings. For example, we can say, "He knew the street was dangerous. He felt uneasy as he walked alone at night."

Find the meaning of the underlined words from the sentences that follow. Circle the best answer.

1. My friends like to <u>travel</u>. Last week they were in Hong Kong. I prefer to stay here in my own city on my vacation.

   Travel most likely means _____.

   a. study   b. go places   c. exercise

2. I was very <u>anxious</u>. I walked up and down. I smoked a cigarette. I sweated.

   Anxious most likely means _____.

   a. happy   b. busy   c. nervous

3. We wanted to go <u>outside</u>, but our mother told us to stay in the house because it was raining.

   Outside most likely means _____.

   a. in a building   b. out of a building   c. near a building

4. The math problem was very <u>complicated</u>. I couldn't do it, and my teacher couldn't do it either.

   Complicated most likely means _____.

   a. easy   b. interesting   c. difficult

5. The story didn't <u>make</u> any <u>sense</u>. I read it four times and I still didn't understand it.

   Make sense most likely means _____.

   a. understandable   b. interesting   c. difficult

Read

4 Read the narrative. Try to understand the meanings of new words without using a dictionary.

A Dream Narrative

[A] This is the dream of a 40-year-old businessman from Chicago. He is married and has two children. He is visiting a psychologist because he feels anxious a lot. The psychologist told him to write down his dreams. This is his dream from June 7.

[B] Dream 6/7:

In my dream I was in a large city. It was very big and very dark. The city seemed like New York, but it didn't look like the real New York. I was in a friend's apartment. While I was in the apartment, I was comfortable. After a few minutes, I left it and went out on the street alone. I walked for a while. Then I realized I was lost. I couldn't find my friend's apartment again. I started to feel uncomfortable and uneasy. I tried to return to the apartment but all of the streets looked unfamiliar and completely different, and I didn't know my friend's address. I began to feel anxious.

[C]   I kept walking. I wanted to find something familiar. It was getting late. I decided to go home. I knew my home was outside the city. On the street I saw buses, but I didn't know which one to take. I couldn't find a way to leave the city. There was a way to get home, but I didn't know it. I asked for directions. The people answered, but they didn't make any sense. All their directions were very complicated, and I couldn't understand them.

[D]   Suddenly I was on a boat. The boat was traveling across a very rough, windy river. It was dark. The river was very dirty—there was garbage in it. I could not see the other side of the river, and I was afraid. I began to think, "I'll never get home." I tried to ask for help, but no one listened to me. Then I woke up.

After You Read

5 **Following Directions.**   Circle the noun that the underlined pronoun is talking about.

1. The (city) seemed like New York, but <u>it</u> didn't look like the real New York.

2. While I was in the apartment, I was comfortable. After a few minutes, I left <u>it</u>.

3. On the street I saw buses, but I didn't know which <u>one</u> to take.

4. There was a way to get home, but I didn't know <u>it</u>.

5. All their directions were very complicated, and I couldn't understand <u>them</u>.

6 **Identifying and Using Verbs.**   Find every subject and verb in the dream narrative that you just read. How many verbs are there? How many are in the simple past tense? What other forms of the verb can you find?

As we learned in Chapter 5, a narrative is like a story. When you write a report about an accident you use a narrative. A salesperson writing about the week's activities uses a narrative. Short stories and novels are other examples of narratives. We make the time clear in a narrative by carefully choosing forms of the past tense. As you can see in the dream narrative you just read, simple narratives use mostly the simple past tense. (You may also need to use the past form of a modal—for example, *can/could*—"I couldn't find my friend's apartment again.") If you use another form of the verb, make sure you know exactly why you are using it. In narratives we sometimes use the past continuous tense. Look at the following examples from "A Dream Narrative."

It <u>was getting</u> late.

The boat <u>was traveling</u> across a very rough, windy river.

We use the past continuous tense for a repeated action in the past or for something that is happening "in the background." This tense uses *was* or *were* + the *-ing* form of the main verb. Can you think of any other examples of the past continuous tense? Share them with the class.

We also use adverbs, phrases, and clauses to make the time in a narrative clear.

Examples

Adverb: <u>Immediately</u>, I left the building.

Prepositional phrase: <u>After a long time</u>, I left the building.

Adverbial time clause: <u>When the TV show ended</u>, I left my apartment.

Read the following sentences from the dream narrative. In each sentence, underline the phrase or word that gives you more information about the time of the action.

Example

<u>Before the TV show ended</u>, I left the apartment.

1. While I was in the apartment, I was comfortable.
2. After a few minutes, I left it.
3. Then I realized I was lost.
4. I walked for a while.
5. Suddenly I was on a boat.

Can you think of other examples? Look in a book or magazine and try to find other examples.

PART 3   Dreams and Their Possible Meanings

1   Many cultures believe that dreams about certain things have special meanings. Many books have been written about the possible meanings of dreams. The following is a list of common dream events and possible interpretations (possible meanings) from these books.

Dream Event	Possible Meaning
a. Your house is on fire.	The house is you. You are feeling strong emotions like anger.
b. Death	A change is coming, or you need to change something in your life.
c. Flying	You feel great freedom, either in your life or your mind.
d. Water (lakes or oceans)	The water is your emotions. If the water is moving and active, then your emotions are moving and active. If the water is still and unmoving, then your emotions are not coming out—you need to tell someone about your emotions.
e. Someone is chasing or following you.	Something or someone in your life is a problem or a danger.
f. Snakes	A snake loses its skin and gets a new skin. This may mean a new life or new career for you.
g. Vampires	Something or someone in your life is stealing your energy.
h. Nakedness (you are not wearing clothes)	If you are frightened or scared, you may have a fear of showing your feelings.
i. Recurring dreams	Your mind is trying to tell you about a problem that needs attention.

Answer the questions. Discuss your answers with a partner.

1.   Are any of the meanings from the list similar to beliefs about dreams in your culture? Which ones?

2.   Do you agree or disagree with the possible meanings? Why or why not?

3.   Do you have dream events like these? What do they mean to you?

2   According to the list, are the following statements true or false? Write T (for *True)* or F (for *False*).

1.   __F__   Dreaming about death may mean someone near to you will die soon.

2.   _____   A recurring dream may mean you have a problem on your mind and you need to do something about this problem.

3.   _____   A dream about a snake means there is danger near you.

4.   _____   A dream about flying may mean you feel very free.

5.   _____   You have a dream. In this dream, you are running naked down Fifth Avenue in New York. This may mean you feel very free and comfortable in cities.

6.   _____   A dream about a peaceful and still ocean is probably good.

7.   _____   In your dream, your house is burning. There is fire everywhere. This is a good dream and it may mean you are excited and happy.

3   Match the dream descriptions with the events from the list in the preceding chart. Write the letter from the list that fits the description.

1.   __h__   I dreamed that I was running down the street but I didn't have any clothes on. I felt embarrassed and frightened.

2.   _____   I have the same dream three or four times a week: I try to drive to work, but my car won't start.

3.   _____   I dreamed that I was sitting in my house and watching TV. I felt very comfortable. Suddenly, my house was on fire.

4.   _____   In my dream, my uncle died (although he is really still alive).

5.   _____   I dreamed that the vampire Dracula came in my window. He had two sharp teeth. He came to my bed.

6.   _____   In my dream, I was like an airplane. I was flying over the city, and the people were very small down below.

7.   _____   I dreamed that I was walking in the park. Suddenly at my feet I saw a huge rattlesnake.

8.   _____   In my dream I was on a boat on the ocean. The water was very still. There was no wind and no movement anywhere.

9.   _____   I dreamed I was walking home from work. Everything was fine. Suddenly a man was behind me. He started running after me. I started running too.

| **PART 4** | # Writing |

Using Sentence Patterns

Two verbs sometimes work together. The first verb can be followed either by an infinitive

> I began <u>to think</u>. ← infinitive

or by a gerund.

> I began <u>thinking</u>. ← gerund

The two sentences mean the same thing.
Here are some other examples.

> I began to feel anxious.
> I began feeling anxious.

> I started to think.
> I started thinking.

Other verbs can *only* be followed by a gerund.

> I kept ~~to think~~. ← infinitive is **not** used
> I kept thinking. ← gerund

Look at "A Dream Narrative" on page 94. Find examples of sentences with verbs followed by infinitives or gerunds. Write the sentences on the following blanks. Use the paragraph letters as a guide.

B

_____

_____

_____

C

_____

_____

_____

D

_____

_____

_____

Now see if the first verb in each sentence can be followed by either an infinitive **or** a gerund, or only by a gerund. Check your answers with the teacher.

Sentence Pattern 7. Some verbs are not like transitive or intransitive verbs. They are more like the verb *be*—they can connect a subject with an adjective or a noun. These verbs are called *linking* verbs.

subject	+	linking verb	+	adjective or noun
George		felt		happy.
George		seemed		sad.
George		became		a teacher.

Linking verbs include

verbs of perception

The house		smelled		strange.
The music		sounded		beautiful.
The girl		looked		pretty.

Many adjectives that follow linking verbs describe positive or negative feelings. Look at the adjectives in the following box. Put them in the Positive or Negative column. (If necessary, use a dictionary to look up the meanings of the adjectives.)

nervous anxious wonderful healthy happy sad comfortable
uncomfortable great depressed lost strange terrible terrific
worried relaxed confident

Positive
wonderful

Negative
nervous

Now list five adjectives to describe the feelings in your dream.

Practicing the Writing Process

1 **Exploring Ideas: Free Writing.**   Write for ten minutes about one of your dreams. Include as many details as you can. Now tell a partner about your dream. Use your freewrite, but don't read it aloud. While you listen to your partner's dream, think about the following two questions:

1. Can you understand the dream? What is it about?
2. Are there interesting details?

Ask your partner questions about his or her dream.

2 **Writing the First Draft.**   Write a first draft of a narrative of your dream. Remember to include the actions, your feelings and what you saw, heard, smelled, tasted, and felt.

3 **Editing.**   Read the student's dream narrative that follows. The student made five errors with the past tense. Can you find them? Correct the errors. Then compare your work with a partner's.

> I dreaming I was in Paris. The city was beautiful and I feeled happy. I could see the Eiffel Tower. I can smell flowers because it was spring. I walkd along a street. A man asks me for directions.

Now check your first draft for errors. Use the following checklist.

Editing Checklist

Does every subject have a verb?

Are your past tense verb forms correct?

Do your sentences begin with capital letters?

Do other words in the writing need capital letters?

Do your sentences end with periods or other final punctuation?

4 **Writing the Second Draft.**   Write your second draft and give it to your teacher.

Writing a Journal

Write a journal entry about something that happened to you. Use the past continuous tense to set the scene. Use adverbs, phrases, and clauses to make the time clear.

> It was very late at night. I was walking home from a party. I opened the door of my apartment. Before I turned on the light, I heard a shriek and I jumped! It was my cat. I stepped on its tail.

Video Activities: Sleep

Before You Watch.

1. How long do most people need to sleep every night?

    a. 6 hours   b. 8 hours   c. 10 hours   d. 12 hours

2. What does our "internal clock" tell us?

    a. when to eat

    b. the time of day

    c. when to sleep and wake up

Watch.

1. How long do young children need to sleep every night?

    a. 6 hours   b. 8 hours   c. 10 hours   d. 12 hours

2. What happens to children who are "sleep deprived" (who don't get enough sleep)? Check all that apply.

    _____ They don't want to get up in the morning.

    _____ They work harder.

    _____ They can't concentrate very well.

    _____ They get into trouble at school.

Watch Again.

1. Check the things that make children stay up later according to the video.

    _____ homework   _____ television   _____ internal clock

    _____ computers   _____ lights   _____ parents

2. How quickly can you change a child's internal clock?

    a. one hour a week   c. one hour a day

    b. two hours a day   d. three hours a week

After You Watch.   Write a paragraph about why our sleep habits changed. One hundred years ago people went to bed earlier and got up earlier. How is life different today than it was 100 years ago? Think about these things: what kind of work did people do? What time did they have to get up? What did they do at nighttime?

Chapter 7

Work and Lifestyles

IN THIS CHAPTER

You will read about people who volunteer to help others. You will also read about the experience of one person who volunteered to help homeless people. You will write a narrative about a work experience.

PART 1

Volunteers

Before You Read

1   Look at the photos and answer the questions with a partner or a group.

1.   Who are these people?
2.   What are they doing? Why?

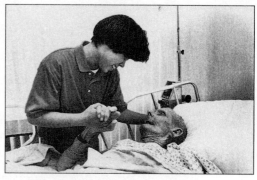

Photo 2

Photo 1

Photo 3

2   **Vocabulary Preview.**   Sometimes a colon (:) can help you understand a new word. If you know the key word or words on one side of the colon, then you can figure out the meaning of the word or words on the other side of the colon.

Examples

There are terrible diseases: AIDS, cancer, and TB.

What are some examples of diseases? _____AIDS, cancer, and TB_____

She cooked some wonderful foods: stews, casseroles, and soufflés.

What are stews, casseroles, and soufflés? _some wonderful foods_

Look at the words before and after the colon in each sentence. Then answer the questions.

1. They look around their neighborhoods and see terrible hardships: sickness, loneliness, and homelessness.

    What are some terrible hardships? _____

2. He started a group, TreePeople, to plant trees: pine, elm, cypress, and eucalyptus.

    What are pine, elm, cypress, and eucalyptus? _____

3. Volunteers help sick ocean mammals: seals, sea lions, and sea otters.

    What are seals, sea lions, and sea otters? _____

Read

3 Read the article.

Volunteers

[A] Some people go to work each day and then come home. They spend time with their family and friends. Maybe they watch TV or go to a movie. Sometimes they exercise or read. This is their life. But for other people, this isn't enough. They look around their neighborhoods and see people with terrible hardships: sickness, loneliness, and homelessness. Other people see problems with the environment. Many people want to help. They volunteer. They give some of their time to help others.

[B]   Volunteers help in many ways. Some visit sick and lonely people. Some give their friendship to children without parents. Some build houses for homeless people. Others sit and hold babies with AIDS.

[C]   Andy Lipkis was at summer camp when he planted his first tree. He began to think about the environment. In many countries, people were cutting down trees. Andy Lipkis worried about this. In 1974, he started a group, TreePeople, to plant trees: pine, elm, cypress, and eucalyptus. Today there are thousands of members of TreePeople, and more join every day. They plant millions of trees everywhere.

[D]   Ruth Brinker wasn't planning to change the world. Then a young friend became sick. He had AIDS. Soon he was very sick, and he couldn't take care of himself. Brinker and other friends began to help him. In 1985, Brinker started Project Open Hand. This group cooks meals and takes them to people with AIDS. Soon Project Open Hand volunteers were cooking 1100 meals every day. This number is growing. Ruth Brinker didn't plan to change the world, but she is making a change in people's lives.

[E]   At the Marine Mammal Center in northern California, volunteers help sick ocean mammals: seals, sea lions, and sea otters. The sick animals become well and strong. Motherless baby animals grow big and healthy. For many weeks—or sometimes months—volunteers help to feed and take care of these ocean animals. They don't get any pay for their hard work. Their "pay" is the good feeling on the day when a healthy animal can return to its home—the ocean.

Cross-Cultural Note

In parts of the United States, one day each spring is National Beach Cleanup Day. Thousands of people volunteer to spend the day at the beach and pick up trash. Is there a custom like this in your country?

[F]   Twenty or thirty years ago, most volunteers were housewives. They volunteered time while their husbands were working. Today both men and women volunteer. There are volunteers from all social classes, all neighborhoods, and all ages. Most aren't rich or famous. They enjoy their volunteer work. People need them. Today, with problems such as AIDS and homelessness, the world needs volunteers more than ever before.

After You Read

4 **Finding the Main Ideas.**   Read the article again. Every paragraph has a letter. What is the main idea of each paragraph? Write the letters on the lines.

   __D__ One woman started a group to take meals to people with AIDS.

   _____ Some people give time each week to help others.

   _____ Volunteers help in different ways.

   _____ Different kinds of people are volunteers.

   _____ One man started a group to plant trees.

   _____ Some people help sick ocean animals.

5 **Making Good Guesses.**   Circle the correct letter to complete the sentence.

   The writer thinks _____.

   a. volunteers are unhappy people

   b. people are afraid of AIDS

   c. volunteers do important work

Discussing the Reading

6 In a small group, answer and discuss the following questions.

   1. What kinds of volunteers are in your country?

   2. Do you volunteer? If so, what do you do? Where do you volunteer?

   3. What volunteer work is interesting to you?

PART 2

A Shelter for the Homeless

Before You Read

1 **Making Predictions.** Look at the pictures. Who are these people? Why are they in this place?

2 **Vocabulary Preview.** Some words end in *-less*. The ending *-less* means "without."

Example

This gum doesn't have sugar. It is ___sugarless___ .

Write a word for each definition (meaning).

1. She doesn't have a home. She is ___homeless___ .

2. He doesn't have a job. He is _____ .

3. They don't have hope. They are _____ .

4. He doesn't have a friend. He is _____ .

5. She didn't get any sleep last night. It was a _____ night.

6. He doesn't have a heart. (He doesn't care about people.) He is

   _____ .

7. The baby sea lion doesn't have a mother. She is _____ .

Read

3 Read the article. If you don't know some words, try to guess their meaning.

A Shelter for the Homeless

[A] Last summer I was a volunteer at a shelter for the homeless, a place for home-less people to sleep at night. I wasn't working that summer. I was taking only two classes in summer school, so I had some free time.

[B]   Three nights a week, I helped in the kitchen of the shelter. With four other volunteers, I planned and cooked a hot dinner for 45 people. We cooked meals with vegetables, chicken, fish, and fruit. The homeless people needed this good food because many of them usually didn't eat well.

[C]   I enjoyed this volunteer work. The other volunteers in the kitchen were in-teresting people. We became friends. One was a very nice elderly housewife. One was a movie actor. Another was a young teacher. And the other was a college student, like me.

[D]   I talked to a lot of the homeless people at the shelter. Some of them told me about their lives. Some had problems with alcohol or drugs. But others only had bad luck. One woman worked for almost 20 years for a small company. Then she lost her job. She looked and looked for a new job, but she couldn't find one. She was too old. She needed money for food, so she sold her furniture—sofas, chairs, and tables. The woman still couldn't find a job. She had no money for her apartment. She had to sleep in her car. Then she had to sell her car. She was alone, afraid, and homeless. Finally, she came to the shelter.

After You Read

4 One word in each sentence is not correct. Cross it out. Then write the correct word.

1. The writer was a volunteer at a shelter for the homeless last ~~winter~~. *summer*

2. With other volunteers, the writer cooked lunch for 45 people.

3. The writer talked to a few of the homeless people at the shelter.

4. All of the homeless people had problems with alcohol or drugs.

5. One woman lost her job after almost ten years with a small company.

5 We use suffixes—word endings—a lot in English. For example, we take the noun *sleep* and add the suffix *-less* (without). The new word—*sleepless*—is an adjective that means "without any sleep." Then we can turn *sleepless* into another noun by adding the suffix *-ness*. The new word—*sleeplessness*—means "the condition of not having any sleep."

Here are some common examples.

1. home   homeless   homelessness
2. hope   hopeless   hopelessness
3. power   powerless   powerlessness

Write the correct form of Nos. 1, 2, and 3 on the following lines.

1. John lost his _____home_____. _____ is a big problem in this city, and he felt very unhappy because he was _____.

2. When people become homeless they often lose _____ for the future. They begin to feel _____. _____ is a big problem for people living in the streets.

3. A person with no money has no _____. This _____ can cause depression and sadness. A homeless person is always a _____ person.

6 **Following Directions.**   Cross out the word that doesn't belong in each group.

1. beautiful   sunny   ~~meet~~   lazy

2. barbecue   diabetes   cancer   disease

3. spend   waste   save   argue

4. happy   homeless   sick   lonely

5. theory   idea   smell   pattern

6. love   believe   marry   think

7. dream   sleep   recurring   food

Cross-Cultural Note

In the 1950s and 1960s in the United States, there were almost no people without homes. Now there are many, many homeless people. Are there more homeless people in your country than in the past? If so, why?

Discussing the Reading

7 Talk about homeless people. Discuss the following questions with the class or in small groups.

1. Are there homeless people in your neighborhood? Are there shelters for the homeless in your neighborhood?

2. What are some reasons for homelessness?

3. Does your country have homeless people? Who helps them?

PART 3   # Work Records

1 Read the following list of volunteer opportunities and write answers to the questions. Then check your answers with a partner.

1. *Elder Care:* Los Angeles Elder Care Corps needs volunteers to visit older people in their homes. Many of these older people seldom have visitors. For information, call Nicky Smith at (213) 555-3444.

2. *Home Building:* Homes for the Needy builds houses for poor families. They are looking for people to paint and work on houses. Call (213) 555-6777.

3. *Summer Camp:* East L. A. Summer Camp for Kids needs volunteers. Volunteers will teach sports and games and help the teachers. Speaking Spanish is useful but not necessary. Please call Ramón Martínez at (213) 555-8999.

4. *Blood Drive:* The American Red Cross needs volunteers. The volunteers will help the nurses. Please call Irene at (213) 555-1112.

1. John helped nurses. What organization did he volunteer for?

   The American Red Cross
   _____

2. Suzy went to old people's homes and talked with the people there. What organization did she volunteer for?

   _____

3. Ted painted houses. What organization did he volunteer for?

   _____

4. Mary helped a teacher during the summer. What organization did she volunteer for?

   _____

2   Read about Ted. Then answer the questions.

Ted Parker worked at three places while he was going to high school. He worked for money at Mike's Market, and he volunteered at the other places. He worked at three places for money while he was going to college. He learned something at every job.

Ted's Work History		
Places	**Dates**	**He Learned . . .**
High School	September, 1997 to June, 2001	
Mike's Market	Jan. 2000–June 2000	He learned to work a cash register.
East L. A. Camp	June 2000–Sept. 2000	He learned to speak some Spanish. He helped the teacher.
Homes for the Needy	June 2002–Sept. 2002	He learned to paint houses.
College	September, 2001 to June, 2005	
Capital Construction Co.	June, 2003 to September, 2003	He learned to use power tools.
Sacramento City College Library	October, 2003 to June, 2004	He learned to use a data base.
Microtel, Inc.	June, 2004 to present	He learned to program computers.

Draw lines to match Ted's job title with the work place.

1. painter

2. supermarket clerk

3. computer programmer

4. teacher's helper

5. construction worker

6. library clerk

a. Microtel, Inc.

b. Sacramento City College Library

c. Mike's Market

d. Homes for the Needy

e. East L. A. Camp

f. Capital Construction Co.

3   A résumé tells about your education and jobs. Here is Ted's résumé. Notice that Ted wrote the earliest dates last. Look at Ted's work history to help you fill in the following blanks.

Theodore William Parker 1341 S. Beaver Avenue Leavit, CA 90042		
Education		
9/01 to 6/05	Sacramento City College	Bachelor of Arts
9/97 to 6/01	U.S. Grant High School	Diploma
9/81 to 6/89	Richard Nixon Elementary School	
Work Experience		
6/96 to present	Microtel, Inc.	Computer programmer
10/03 to 6/04	Sacramento City College Library	Library Clerk
6/03 to 9/03	_____	_____
_____	_____	_____
_____	_____	_____
_____	_____	_____

Now write a résumé for yourself. Use the résumé you just read as a guide.

PART 4   Writing

Using Past Tense Verbs

Look at Paragraphs A and B from the article "A Shelter for the Homeless." How many verbs are in the simple past tense, and how many verbs are in the past continuous?

_____ simple past tense

_____ past continuous tense

Use the article "A Shelter for the Homeless" to help you fill in the missing simple past form of each of the following verbs.

Simple Past

1. write   _____
2. volunteer   _____
3. talk   _____
4. cook   _____
5. sit   _____
6. become   _____
7. meet   _____
8. get   _____
9. tell   _____
10. ask   _____
11. keep   _____
12. decide   _____
13. start   _____
14. know   _____
15. answer   _____
16. seem   _____

Sometimes we are asked to write about a job experience—either as part of an English writing test or for a job application. A good writer always thinks about the person who will read his or her writing—the writer's "audience." For example, if you are writing about your work skills and experience, you want to make a good impression on your audience. Read the following job experience narrative. Like many students, the writer had a problem. She was only 20 years old and had no formal job experience because she had always been a student. But notice that she found an important job to write about anyhow.

[A]   The most important job I ever had was taking care of my little sister. From the time I was five or six, I took care of her. Both my parents worked, and I was like a mother to her. I had to dress her and feed her, watch over her, and keep her out of danger. This was a lot of responsibility for a young girl, and there were times when I just wanted to go out and play and forget about my sister. But I knew I couldn't do this.

[B]   My job was difficult, but I learned some important things. First, I learned responsibility. I always do my schoolwork now because I learned to be responsible. Also, I learned how difficult it is to raise a child. I plan to wait until I finish college before I get married and have a child.

What verb tenses did the writer use and why? Compare your answers with a partner's.

Practicing the Writing Process

1   **Exploring Ideas: Free Writing.**   You are going to write about one of your work experiences. To get some general ideas down on paper, complete the following sentences. Don't worry about spelling or correct grammar.

1. My most important work experience was _____

    _____

2. At this job, I _____

    _____

3. From this job, I learned _____

    _____

Now think of some details about your work experience that will make your narrative interesting. For example, think of specific information. Write down these details in the spaces after the following questions. Again, don't worry about spelling, grammar, or punctuation.

What exactly did you do on this job?

_____

_____

How did the job make you feel?

_____

_____

What difficulties were there?

_____

_____

What did the workplace look like?

_____

_____

What were the people you worked with like?

_____

_____

What did you like most about the job?

_____

_____

2 **Writing the First Draft.** Write your first draft of your job experience narrative.

3 **Editing.** Did you use any of the verbs in Using Past Tense Verbs in your first draft? Most of the verbs in your narrative should be in the simple past tense. Check your verbs. Are they in the simple past? Are they regular or irregular? Is the form correct?

Edit your first draft. Then show your work to a partner. Does your partner have any comments? Are any of your work experiences the same?

Use the following checklist to correct any mistakes.

Editing Checklist

Are your past tense verb forms correct?

Does every subject have a verb?

Do your sentences begin with capital letters?

Do other words in the writing need capital letters?

Do your sentences end with periods or other final punctuation?

4 **Writing the Second Draft.** Now write your second draft and give it to your teacher.

Writing a Journal

Write a journal entry about a time you helped someone with a task. For example, helping a younger brother or sister assemble a toy, helping a relative in a business, or helping around the house. Use the simple past tense verbs in Part 4 if you can.

After my uncle's house was flooded, I helped him clean the first floor. We moved the furniture outside. We dried the floors with mops and rags. We cleaned the walls.

Video Activities: Dentist Fashion Designer

Before You Watch.

1. Match the careers in A with the descriptions in B.

   A   **B**

   a. fashion designer   a. takes pictures

   b. dentist   b. paints pictures

   c. photographer   c. makes clothes

   d. artist   d. fixes teeth

2. Which of the preceding careers is different from the others? Why?

Watch.   Check all the correct answers.

1. Steve Schneider is a

   a. dentist.   b. photographer.   c. fashion designer.

2. Steve Schneider _____

   a. _____ likes dentistry as much as fashion design.

   b. _____ doesn't like having two careers.

   c. _____ started designing clothes in college.

Watch Again.

1. Steve Chriter has designed clothes for

   _____ Arnold Schwarzennegger

   _____ Bruce Springsteen

   _____ Tom Cruise

   _____ Sharon Stone

2. Put a D next to the benefit of being a dentist. Put an F next to the
   benefit of being a fashion designer.

   _____ Make more money.

   _____ Talk to people.

   _____ Work alone.

After You Watch.   Read this paragraph about a woman who is an artist and a
doctor. Then use your imagination to write a story about another person with two
careers.

When I was young, I decided to be a doctor. While I was studying medicine, I
started working for an artist. At first, I just answered the telephone and
cleaned up. In my free time, I painted just for fun. Then, one day while I was
painting, a customer came into the studio. She saw my paintings and she
liked them. Soon, I became a part-time artist too.

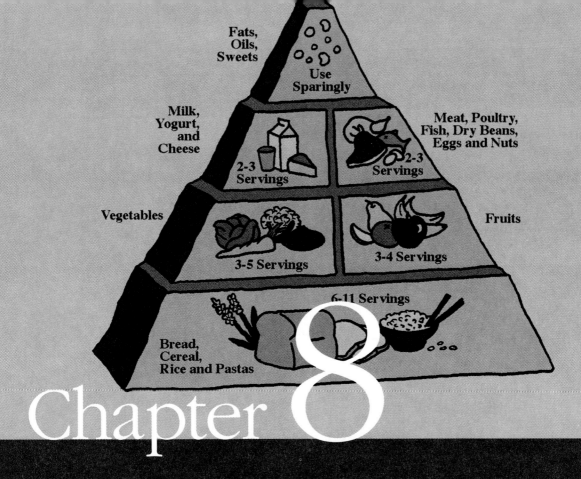

Fats,
Oils,
Sweets

Use
Sparingly

Milk,
Yogurt,
and
Cheese

2-3
Servings

Meat, Poultry,
Fish, Dry Beans,
Eggs and Nuts

2-3
Servings

Vegetables

3-5 Servings

Fruits

3-4 Servings

6-11 Servings

Bread,
Cereal,
Rice and Pastas

Chapter 8

Food and Nutrition

IN THIS CHAPTER

You will read about how people are changing their way of eating. You will read about some strange things people eat, and you'll write about how to do something.

| PART 1 | # New Foods, New Diets |

Before You Read

1   Look at the photos. Discuss the questions with a partner or a group.

1.   How are these two photos different?

2.   In your opinion, what was important to the people in the first photo? What's important to the people in the second photo?

Photo 1

Photo 2

2   **Vocabulary Preview.**   Sometimes you can understand a new word if you know its opposite. *Big* is the opposite of *small*. *Terrible* is the opposite of *wonderful*. If you know one of these words, you may not need a dictionary for the other.

Example

The people in the first photo aren't <u>slender</u>; they're overweight.
The opposite of *slender* is *overweight*.

On the blanks, write the opposites of the underlined words.

1.   People thought, "How <u>attractive</u>!"—not "How ugly!"

The opposite of *attractive* is _____.

2.   Many of the vegetables are <u>raw</u>. They aren't cooked because cooking takes away some vitamins.

The opposite of *raw* is _____.

3.   They want to be <u>slim</u>, not fat.

The opposite of *slim* is _____.

4.   Sometimes people lose weight fast, but they usually <u>gain</u> it again.

The opposite of *gain* is _____.

Match the meanings with the underlined words. Write letters on the lines.

1. _____ pictures

2. _____ not fat or heavy at all

3. _____ what you eat

4. _____ foods from milk and cream

5. _____ a sickness

6. _____ people who paint pictures

a. The dancer was light and <u>slender</u>.

b. Leonardo Da Vinci and Picasso are two famous <u>artists.</u>

c. Many people die from <u>heart disease</u> every year.

d. The <u>paintings</u> were on the wall of the museum.

e. The butter and cheese are in the <u>dairy</u> section.

f. His <u>diet</u> had too much meat and too few vegetables.

Read

3 Read the article. As you read, think about the main ideas of the article.

New Foods, New Diets

[A] On March 26, 1662, Samuel Pepys and four friends had lunch at his home in London, England. They ate beef, cheese, two kinds of fish, and six chickens. They didn't eat any fruits or vegetables. More than 300 years ago, people in Europe ate differently from today. They looked different too. In famous paintings by Titian, Rubens, and other artists, people weren't slender; they were over-weight. But people 300 years ago thought, "How attractive!"—not "How ugly!"

[B] Today people are learning more about health. People in North America and Europe are changing their way of eating. They're eating a lot of fruits and vegetables. Many of the vegetables are raw. They aren't cooked because cooking takes away some vitamins, such as vitamins A, B, and C. People are eating less sugar. They're not eating much red meat. They're drinking less cola and coffee. They're eating low-fat foods.

[C] People these days want to be slender, not fat. Sometimes people in North America go a little crazy to lose pounds. Thousands of them join diet groups, go to special diet doctors, or spend a lot of money at diet centers. Each year Americans spend more than $30 billion on diets and diet products. Sometimes people lose weight fast, but they usually gain it back again. Almost 95 percent of all people gain back weight after a diet.

[D] Diets are changing in many countries, but this isn't always good news. For example, the Japanese diet was very healthful for many years. People ate a lot of fish and vegetables. Now they're eating more and more beef, sugar, and dairy products—ice cream and cheese. This seems similar to Samuel Pepys's party, doesn't it? The problem with this change in diet is easy to see. There is more sickness such as heart disease. The changing diet is not good for the health of the Japanese people.

[E] Sometimes people go crazy over food. They eat lots of bad foods because they taste good. Or, other times, they do the opposite—eat very little because they want to be slender. When will people learn? Too much food, too little food, and the wrong foods are all bad ideas.

Cross-Cultural Note

Vegetarians are people that eat no meat. Some vegetarians don't eat dairy products, either. In what countries or cultures is it easy to be a vegetarian? In what countries or cultures is it hard? If you are a vegetarian, why did you decide to be one? If you are not a vegetarian, would you consider becoming one?

After You Read

4   **Finding the Main Ideas.**   Circle the number of the main idea of "New Foods, New Diets."

1. It's important to eat fruits and vegetables.

2. People today eat differently from people in the past.

3. People in the past were fat; people today are not fat.

4. The way of eating today is better than in the past.

5   Read "New Foods, New Diets" again. Every paragraph has a letter. What is the main idea of each paragraph? Write the letters on the lines.

___E___   People sometimes go crazy over food.

_____   Europeans in the past ate differently from today, and they were overweight.

_____   The Japanese way of eating is changing, but the change isn't good.

_____   The way of eating in Europe and North America is changing.

_____   Today Americans don't want to be overweight. They do many things to lose weight.

6   **Making Good Guesses.**   Circle the correct letter to complete the sentence.

The author (writer) of "New Foods, New Diets" probably _____.

a. doesn't like crazy diets

b. eats a lot of meat, sugar, and dairy products

c. is a member of a diet group

Discussing the Reading

7   Talk about your answers to the following questions with a partner.

1. How much meat do you eat? How often do you eat fruits and vegetables?

2. What do people eat in your country? Fill in the chart on page 121.

	United States		Your Country
Breakfast	cereal	ham	
	juice or	eggs	
	coffee	toast	
	fruit	coffee	
Lunch	sandwich	soup	
	salad or	salad	
	milk	bread	
Dinner	chicken		
	green vegetables		
	potato		
	fruit		
	ice cream		

PART 2   # Eating Bugs

Before You Read

1   **Vocabulary Preview.**   The suffix *-able* is often added to a verb and the resulting adjective means "able to (verb)."

Example
You can drink this water because it's safe. It is ___*drinkable*_____ .

For the underlined verb, write the adjective that means "able to . . ."

1.   You can <u>eat</u> this food. It is safe. It is _____ .

2.   You can <u>afford</u> to buy something. It is _____ .

3.   You can <u>enjoy</u> something. It is _____ .

4.   You can <u>predict</u> something (know it is going to happen in the future). It is

_____ .

5.   You can <u>notice</u> (see) something. It is _____ .

6.   People <u>remark</u> (talk) about something because it is unusual. It is

_____ .

Sometimes if you know one of two opposites you can guess the other.

Example

Some people think this food is delicious—that it tastes very good; others think it is disgusting.

Disgusting probably means <u>tastes very bad</u>.

Write answers in the blanks.

1. Some of the foods were crisp and hard, others were soft and gooey.

   Gooey probably means _____.

2. These insects don't have ears like humans—they have four-inch long antennas.

   Antennas probably means _____.

3. Some people were jumping into the water, while other people were diving into it.

   Diving probably means _____.

4. Some people know nothing about bugs, but entomologists are experts.

   The word *experts* probably means _____.

Work with a partner or in a group. Look at the pictures. Label the different kinds of insects with the words from the box. Use your dictionary if necessary.

bees	crickets	mealworms	grasshoppers
caterpillars	water bugs	larva	beetles

1. _____   2. _____   3. _____   4. _____

5. _____   6. _____   7. _____   8. _____

Read

2 Read the article. Try to guess the meanings of words you don't know.

Eating Bugs

[A] Different cultures like different foods, and sometimes a food that one culture thinks is delicious will seem disgusting to another. Dr. Louis Sorkin knows this because he eats insects, and almost every culture thinks at least something he eats is disgusting. Dr. Sorkin not only eats insects, he enjoys them.

[B]   Sorkin is an entomologist. Entomologists study insects, and he is studying eatable insects. He knows of at least 500 insect species that people eat somewhere in the world. Last year Sorkin ate baby bees, crickets, mealworms, grasshoppers and caterpillars as well as many other insects. "People eat insects all over the world," he says. "In Asia, Africa, South America and Mexico."

[C]   Some people in Asia, for example, eat giant water bugs. They boil them like Americans and Europeans boil lobster. These bugs are so big they can eat fish. Another entomologist described eating these bugs: "You eat the abdomen—the stomach area—first. It's kind of soft and gooey and has a strong taste. It can give you a terrible case of bad breath!"

[D]   Bugs can taste very good, says another insect expert. "One of my favorites is the wax moth larva. It's an inch-long caterpillar. Drop it into a deep-fat fryer for 40 seconds, and it pops like popcorn. It tastes a lot like bacon."

[E]   People don't usually eat bugs in Europe or North America, but they did at one time. The ancient Greeks cooked cicadas (an insect like a grasshopper) and the Romans ate wood-boring beetles. The American Indians also ate bugs. They ate grasshoppers, crickets, and caterpillars. Once we are used to certain foods, our tastes can be very different. Hindus in India are disgusted by eating beef, and many Asians think cheese is pretty horrible. Americans find it strange that many French eat horsemeat and frogs.

[F]   As the world becomes more international, food tastes are getting wider in many countries. Americans now eat Japanese sushi (raw fish) and French snails. Maybe someday Americans will say, "Give me a hamburger and an order of water beetles, please."

After You Read

3   **Finding the Main Ideas.**   Circle the number of the main idea of "Eating Bugs."

1. Eating bugs is disgusting to many people.

2. Some people eat insects because they are poor.

3. Different people have different tastes in food.

Remember that a topic sentence is the sentence in a paragraph that gives the main idea of the paragraph. Often it is the first sentence in the paragraph, but not always. The first sentence of Paragraph A is the topic sentence. Underline the topic sentence in the other paragraphs. Now share you work with a partner or a group. Did you pick the same topic sentences?

The first paragraph of an information text often states a main idea. Often it also tries to get your attention by saying something unusual or by asking a question. What is unusual—gets your attention—in the first paragraph of "Eating Bugs"? Share your answer with a partner.

Something related to the main idea of a paragraph is its purpose. Read "Eating Bugs" again. This time try to understand the purpose of each paragraph. Each purpose is listed here. Which paragraphs do they belong to? Write the correct paragraph letters on the lines.

_____   This paragraph makes a conclusion, like saying "good-bye" to the reader.

_____   This paragraph tells the history of insect eating in Europe and America, and also gives us an example of the main idea in Paragraph A.

_____   This paragraph gives us an example of a bug people eat.

_____   This paragraph tells us who Dr. Sorkin is and why he is eating bugs.

_____   This paragraph gives a second example of a bug people eat.

_____   This paragraph introduces us to Dr. Sorkin.

4 **Following Directions.**   Complete the sentences. Circle the best answer. There is only one best answer for each blank.

1. An entomologist studies _____.

   a. water beetles   c. insects

   b. birds   d. words

2. _____ do not eat beef.

   a. Indians   c. Hindus

   b. Insects   d. Moroccans

3. Sushi is _____ fish.

   a. Chinese   c. fried

   b. cooked   d. raw

4. People lose weight to become _____.

   a. fat   c. anxious

   b. sad   d. slender

5. We may sleep to save _____.

   a. energy   c. homelessness

   b. time   d. money

6. They fell in love and _____ married.

   a. did   c. got

   b. made   d. had

7. If you borrow money, you need to _____ it back.

   a. waste   c. pay

   b. lend   d. make

Discussing the Reading

5 Do you eat anything that people from other cultures sometimes think is strange? What is the strangest food you ever ate? Share your information with a partner or a small group.

PART 3	**Fat and Calories**

1 Look at the following chart. It lists the fat and calories in a few foods.

Food	Calories	Fat (in grams)
1. beef steak (3 oz.)	242	14.7
2. broccoli (3 1/2 oz.)	25	.2
3. chicken (baked leg)	130	4.7
4. cookies (1)	57	3.3
5. French fries (8 large)	200	10.0
6. grapes (1 bunch)	51	.1
7. milk (1 glass)	149	8.1
8. tomato juice (small glass)	41	.1

Here is Bill's dinner. Look at the
picture and answer the questions.
Use the calorie and fat chart.

3 oz. steak   french fries
cookies   milk

1. How many calories does Bill's
    steak have?

    Bill's steak has 242 calories.

2. How much fat does it have? (How many grams of fat?)

    _____

3. How many calories do Bill's french fries have?

    _____

4. How much fat do they have? (How many grams?)

    _____

5. How many calories does Bill's complete meal have?

    _____

6.   How much fat does it have? (How many grams?)

_____

7.   Bill's doctor wants Bill to eat about 500 calories for dinner. Does Bill's dinner have 500 calories, or does it have more than 500 calories?

_____

Here is Maria's dinner. Look at the picture and then answer the questions. Use the calorie and fat chart.

baked chicken leg broccoli
tomato juice grapes

1.   How many calories does Maria's chicken have?

_____

_____

2.   How much fat does it have? (How many grams of fat?)

_____

3.   How many calories do Maria's grapes have?

_____

4.   How much fat do they have? (How many grams)?

_____

5.   How many calories does Maria's complete dinner have?

_____

6.   How much fat does it have? (How many grams?)

_____

7.   You want to lose weight. Should you eat Maria's dinner or Bill's dinner?

_____

8.   You want to eat less fat. Should you eat Bill's dinner or Maria's dinner?

_____

2 Use the chart of healthy weights to answer the questions that follow.

	Men				Women		
Height	Weight in pounds			**Height**	Weight in pounds		
	Small frame	Medium frame	Large frame		Small frame	Medium frame	Large frame
5'3"	118	129	141	5'0"	100	109	118
5'4"	122	133	145	5'1"	104	112	121
5'5"	126	137	149	5'2"	107	115	125
5'6"	130	142	155	5'3"	110	118	128
5'7"	134	147	161	5'4"	113	122	132
5'8"	139	151	166	5'5"	116	125	135
5'9"	143	155	170	5'6"	120	129	139
5'11"	150	163	178	5'8"	126	136	146
6'0"	154	167	183	5'9"	130	140	151
6'1"	158	171	188	5'10"	133	144	156
6'2"	162	175	192	5'11"	137	148	161
6'3"	165	178	195	6'0"	141	152	166

Small frame   Medium frame   Large frame

1. Tony is 5'7". He has a large frame. How much should he weigh?

   _____

2. Carmen is 5'8". She has a small frame. How much should she weigh?

   _____

3. Dena has a large frame. She is 5'3". How much should she weigh?

   _____

4. Daniel weighs 150 pounds. He has a small frame. He is 5'8". Is he underweight, just right, or overweight?

   _____

5. Manya weighs 122 pounds. She is 5'4". She has a medium frame. Is she underweight, just right, or overweight?

   _____

6. How about you?

   _____

PART 4

Writing

Using the Command Form of Verbs

Here are a student's directions about how to do something. It is a recipe. Before you read it, find out what these words mean—*swirl, stir, flip*. Ask your teacher, other students, or look in your dictionary.

How to Stir-Fry Chicken

The ingredients are chicken (cut into small pieces), chopped garlic, and ginger.

First heat a wok (a Chinese frying pan) or other frying pan until hot. Next add 2 tablespoons of oil and swirl the oil around to cover the surface of the pan. Heat until hot. Then turn the heat to medium, put in the ginger and garlic, and stir a few times. Now turn the heat to high and put in the chicken, stirring it quickly around in the pan. Keep turning it and flipping it with a spatula for about one minute or until it is white. Finally, add the seasoning sauce. (The seasoning sauce is 2 tablespoons of soy sauce mixed with a tablespoon of sugar and four tablespoons of Chinese rice wine.)

When we write about how to do something (describe a process), we often use what is called the "command form" of the verb. It is the simple or infinitive form of the verb. The subject of this verb—*you*—is not stated. We give commands (directions) with only the verb.

(subject)	+	**verb**	
(*you*—not stated)		Turn	the heat to medium.

Underline all the command forms in the recipe "How to Stir-Fry Chicken." Then check your answers with a partner.

Also, when we describe a process, we usually use sequence words such as *first, second, third,* and so on, or *next, now, then,* and *finally* to indicate or signal the steps in the process. Underline all the sequence words in the recipe. What kind of word comes immediately after them? Share your answers with a partner.

Practicing the Writing Process

1 **Exploring Ideas: Free Writing.**   You are going to write directions about how to do something. You can write about preparing a special food from your country or about something else you know how to do, such as wash a car, make a dress, or fix a broken window. First decide what process you want to write about. Then write for ten minutes about how to do it—the basic steps. Don't worry about spelling, grammar, or punctuation. Imagine you are telling someone how to do the steps. Just write down as many steps as you can think of.

2 **Writing the First Draft.**   Write your first draft. Begin by reviewing your freewrite. Make sure all the steps are there and in the correct sequence.

3 **Editing.**   Now check your work. Use the following list to help correct any mistakes.

Editing Checklist

Are the verb forms correct—are most of them in the simple (command) form?

Are there sequence words to signal the steps?

Do your sentences begin with capital letters?

Do other words in the writing need capital letters?

Do your sentences end with periods or other final punctuation?

4 **Writing the Second Draft.**   Write your second draft and hand it in to your teacher.

Video Activities: Diets

Before You Watch.

1. People on diets usually want to

    a. lose weight.   b. gain weight.   c. get stronger.

2. Check the foods that people on restrictive diets usually cannot eat.

    _____ ice cream   _____ candy

    _____ vegetables   _____ bread

    _____ fruit   _____ butter

    _____ chicken   _____ rice

Watch.

> Vocabulary Note:
> A crash diet is very restrictive. People on crash diets are usually trying to lose weight very quickly.

1. Dr. Goodrick explains why restrictive diets are

    a. good for you.

    b. dangerous.

    c. necessary for some people.

2. Check all of the things that Dr. Goodrick says a crash diet can do:

    _____ change your brain chemistry

    _____ help you stay thin

    _____ make you want to eat more

    _____ make you gain weight

Watch Again.

1. How long should it take to get used to a low-fat diet?

    a. almost 6 weeks   b. at least 6 months   c. about 6 days

2. Check all of the things that you should do to lose weight:

    _____ eat only fruits and vegetables

    _____ change your eating habits slowly

    _____ eat fewer than 1200 calories a day

    _____ find friends to help you

    _____ try new ways of cooking

    _____ stop eating high-fat foods immediately

    _____ plan your meals

    _____ exercise

After You Watch.   You just received a letter from a friend. Your friend is on a crash diet. She is only eating tuna fish and grapefruit. Complete the letter with information from the video.

Dear _____,

I just saw an interesting program about losing weight. The doctor said that crash diets are not good. Here are some reasons why you shouldn't go on a crash diet.

   Here is the doctor's advice about losing weight safely.

Chapter 9

Great Destinations

IN THIS CHAPTER

You'll read about exciting adventure vacations. You'll play a game to find out what kind of vacation is perfect for you, and you'll write a letter to a friend about a great vacation.

Adventure Vacations

Before You Read

1 Look at the three photos. Then answer the following questions. Discuss your answers with a partner or a group.

1. What are these people doing?
2. What do you like to do on a vacation?

2 **Vocabulary Preview.**   We often use *go + -ing* to describe activities we do for plea-sure. For example, we use *go + swimming* to describe the complete activity of going to a place and swimming. Rather than saying "Let's swim" to suggest the activity, we usually say "Let's go swimming." We also often add the verb *be + going to* before *go + -ing*: "We're going to go swimming." This expresses an action that will take place in the future.

Example

The verb *swim* means "to use one's body to move through the water." But if someone asks you, "What are you going to do tomorrow?" you probably wouldn't say, "I'm going to swim." Instead you would answer, "I'm going to

*go swimming*_____."

Complete the following sentences. Then check your answers with a partner.

1. The verb *camp* means "to live for a while in a temporary place, usually in a tent." But if someone asks you, "What are going to do this summer?" you would answer,

    "I'm going to _____."

2. The verb *sightsee* means "to take a trip to a place and look around," in other words, to "see the sights at a place that a person specially travels to." But if someone asks you, "What are you going to do in Mexico?" you would probably answer,

    "_____."

Here are some other common verbs with *go*—*go hiking, go walking, go jogging, go boating, go surfing, go bowling, go window-shopping, go fishing*. If you don't know the meanings of some of these verbs, ask a classmate or your teacher. Then work with a partner and practice using these verbs in sentences.

3 **Making Good Guesses.**   Remember that sometimes you can understand new words without a dictionary. For example, you can figure out or guess the meanings from other words in the sentence. Guess the meaning of the underlined words. Circle the letter to complete the sentence.

1. When I visited London I went to the Tate Museum, but there were so many other <u>tourists</u> there, I couldn't see anything. It was hot and crowded.

    Tourists are most likely _____.

    a. police officers   b. sightseers   c. art experts

2. Many things cause <u>pollution</u>—for example, factory smoke, car exhaust, trash, and garbage.

   Pollution is most likely _____.

   a. rain and bad weather

   b. a lot of new business

   c. bad things in the air and environment

3. The mountain was really a <u>volcano</u>. Twenty years ago smoke and fire poured out of the top of the mountain.

   A volcano is most likely a _____.

   a. mountain with ice at the top

   b. mountain with a hole in the top

   c. mountain that is very tall

Read

4 Read the article. Try to guess the meanings of new words.

Adventure Vacations

[A] People like different kinds of vacations. Some go camping. They swim, fish, cook over a fire, and sleep outside. Others like to stay at a hotel in an exciting city. They go shopping all day and go dancing all night. Or maybe they go sightseeing to places such as Disneyland, the Taj Mahal, or the Louvre.

[B]   Some people are bored with sightseeing trips. They don't want to be "tourists." They want to have an adventure—a surprising and exciting trip. They want to learn something and maybe help people too. How can they do this? Some travel companies and environmental groups are planning special adventures. Sometimes these trips are difficult and full of hardships, but they're a lot of fun. One organization, Earthwatch, sends small groups of volunteers to different parts of the world. Some volunteers spend two weeks and study the environment. Others work with animals. Others learn about people of the past.

[C]   Would you like an adventure in the Far North? A team of volunteers is leaving from Murmansk, Russia. The leader of this trip is a professor from Alaska. He's worried about chemicals from factories. He and the volunteers will study this pollution in the environment. If you like exercise and cold weather, this is a good trip for you. Volunteers need to ski 16 kilometers every day.

[D]   Do you enjoy ocean animals? You can spend two to four weeks in Hawaii. There, you can teach language to dolphins. Dolphins can follow orders such as "Bring me the large ball." They also understand opposites. How much more can they understand? It will be exciting to learn about these intelligent animals. Another study trip goes to Washington State and follows orcas. We call orcas "killer whales," but they're really dolphins—the largest kind of dolphin. These beautiful animals travel together in family groups. They move through the ocean with their mothers, grandmothers, and great-grandmothers. Ocean pollution is changing their lives. Earthwatch is studying how this happens.

[E]   Are you interested in history? Then Greece is the place for your adventure. Thirty-five hundred years ago a volcano exploded there, on Santorini. This explosion was more terrible than Krakatoa or Mount Saint Helens. But today we know a lot about the way of life of the people from that time. There are houses, kitchens, and paintings as interesting as those in Pompeii. Today teams of volunteers are learning more about people from the past.

[F]   Do you want a very different vacation? Do you want to travel far, work hard, and learn a lot? Then an Earthwatch vacation is for you.

After You Read

5   **Finding the Main Ideas.**   Circle the number of the main idea of "Adventure Vacations."

1. An adventure with Earthwatch is a good way to learn something and have a vacation too.

2. It's more fun to stay at a hotel than to go camping.

3. Disneyland, the Taj Mahal, and the Louvre are wonderful places to see on a vacation.

4. Earthwatch trips are difficult and full of hardships.

Here are the main ideas of Paragraphs A to D. What information about the main idea is in each paragraph? Put checks on the lines.

A: People like different kinds of vacations.

___✔___ Some people go camping.

_____ Some people swim, fish, cook over a fire, and sleep outside.

_____ Some people stay at a hotel in a city.

_____ Some people learn about neighborhood problems.

_____ Some people go shopping and dancing.

_____ Some people go to special places such as Disneyland.

B: Some people want an adventure.

_____ They want to stay at a hotel and go shopping.

_____ They want to learn something and maybe help people too.

_____ Some groups plan special adventures.

_____ Earthwatch sends volunteers to different places in the world.

_____ Earthwatch volunteers help in shelters for the homeless.

_____ Earthwatch volunteers study the environment, work with animals, and learn about people of the past.

C: A group of volunteers is going to study pollution in the arctic.

_____ The leader is a professor from Murmansk.

_____ The professor is worried about chemicals.

_____ People on this trip will go camping.

_____ People on this trip will ski 16 kilometers every day.

D: You can teach dolphins in Hawaii or study orcas in Washington.

_____ Dolphins can follow orders.

_____ Dolphins understand opposites.

_____ Dolphins are intelligent.

_____ Dolphins are fish.

_____ Orcas travel in family groups.

_____ Pollution is changing the lives of orcas.

6   **Making Good Guesses.**   Circle the correct letter to complete the sentence.

The writer probably _____.

a.   likes to go sightseeing

b.   likes adventures

c.   teaches language to dolphins

Discussing the Reading

7   Talk about your answers in small groups.

1.   What do you like to do for fun in your free time?

2.   Do you sometimes go camping? If so, where?

3.   Do you like to go shopping, dancing, or sightseeing? If so, where?

4.   Do you enjoy museums? If so, which ones do you like?

5.   Would you like an adventure? If so, what kind of adventure? Are any of the adventures in Paragraphs C, D, and E interesting to you? Why, or why not?

Cross-Cultural Note

Some Canadians and Americans "relax" by spending their vacations as volunteers. They work hard on their vacation, but it's different from their usual job, and they enjoy it. What are some popular vacations in your country?

| PART 2 | **The Travel Quiz** |

Before You Read

1 **Making Predictions.**   Look at the photos that follow about different kinds of vacations. What type of person might enjoy each vacation?

a.

Be a part of it! See New York!

c.

Explore the Coral Reef.

Go deep-sea diving
in the Caribbean Sea.

b.

Visit the Grand Tetons.

2   Which of the three vacations would you like? Write your answer on a piece of paper, not in your book. Don't tell anyone your answer!

Read

3 Read and take the following test. Circle your answers. (You'll get more information after the test.)

1. What do you like to do in the morning?

   a. sleep late   b. exercise   c. watch TV

2. What do you like to do on Saturday and Sunday?

   a. go fishing   b. go swimming   c. go shopping

3. What's most interesting to study when you're on vacation?

   a. nothing   b. animals   c. paintings in a museum

4. What do you not enjoy?

   a. a busy, crowded city   b. being cold   c. sleeping outside

5. It's boring to _____.

   a. spend the day at the ocean

   b. go shopping all day

   c. do nothing

6. What gives you a headache?

   a. hot weather   b. smoke from buses   c. cold air

7. What's most important?

   a. clean water   b. clean air   c. a clean bathroom

8. The best food is _____.

   a. cooked over a campfire

   b. fresh seafood

   c. in a good restaurant

9. I like a vacation to be _____.

   a. quiet, with no worries

   b. exciting, with adventure

   c. exciting, with lots of people

10. Which activity do you like best?

    a. relaxing   b. water sports   c. sightseeing

After You Read

4   **Making Good Guesses.**   Now exchange books with a partner and read each other's answers. What can you guess about your partner? In other words, which vacation did your partner choose (1, 2, or 3)?

Discussing the Reading

5   Look again at your partner's answers on the test. Give your partner suggestions. (For example: "You like cities. Maybe you should go to Hong Kong. It's exciting." Or: "Lake Louise is beautiful. You'll like it.")

6   **Building Vocabulary.**   Which word in each group doesn't belong? Cross it out.

1. psychiatrist   Sigmund Freud   ~~culture~~   psychologist

2. grasshopper   sushi   larva   bee

3. exciting   shopping   dancing   sightseeing

4. organization   team   professor   group

5. eggs   toast   fruit   vitamin

6. taste   smell   eat   see

Are the meanings of the following words similar, different, or opposite? Write S (similar), D (different), or O (opposite) on the lines.

1. __O__ exciting—boring

2. _____ dolphins—orcas

3. _____ weather—ocean

4. _____ mountain—lake

5. _____ same—different

6. _____ disgusting—delicious

7. _____ random—organized

Read the words about travel and the environment in the box. Work with a partner. Fill in the squares of the crossword puzzle with the following words.

tourist	trees	trip	travel
adventure	vacation	mountains	orcas
volcano	ocean	pollution	stars

Across

 1. an exciting trip
 5. time without working (usually 1–2 weeks)
 7. high places (such as the Alps, the Andes, and the Himalayas)
10. green things (such as elm, pine, and cypress)
11. "killer whales" or large dolphins
12. a time of travel from one place to another

Down

 2. a mountain with fire in it
 3. If water and air are not clean, there is _____.
 4. a person on a sightseeing trip
 6. to go on a trip
 8. a large area of water (such as the Pacific or the Atlantic)
 9. We see them at night, outside, if we look up.

PART 3

Tours and Using a Travel Map

1   Look at the photos and read about the different tours that follow. Don't worry about new words. Then answer the questions that follow.

Adventure Tours, Inc.

Do you want something different? Something exciting? Here is our new group of tours.

1. Tibet Tour

Six days in one of the most unusual counties in Asia. Very few tourists go to Tibet. All around are the tallest mountains in the world. You will visit beautiful monasteries and crowded street markets. You will also see wonderful Tibetan dancing.

Length of trip: 14 days. Group size: 16
Cost: $6,000

2. Maui Bicycling Tour

Ride a bicycle around the most beautiful tropical island in the world. You will swim in the clear, warm tropical water, and go camping in the beautiful national parks.

Length of trip: 7 days. Group size: 9–12
Cost: $695

3. Cooking Tour

Do you like French food? Do you like to cook? Visit Paris and seven other French cities. Visit the best restaurants. Eat the most delicious food in the world. Study cooking with the most interesting chefs of France.

Length of trip: 15 days. Group size: 14–18
Cost: $4,500

3. American River Trip

California's American River is one of the fastest, most exciting, and most difficult rivers to raft. You will never forget this trip! The trip is for adventurous people only! You must be in good health.

Length of trip: 3 days. Group size: 8–10
Cost: $650

1. Which tour is the most expensive?

    Tour 1 is most expensive.
    _____

2. Which tour is the longest?

    _____

3. Which tour is the most dangerous?

    _____

Answer the following questions. There are no right or wrong answers.

1. Which tour is the most interesting?

    _____

2. Which tour is the most exciting?

    _____

3. Which tour is the best?

    _____

Now read what different people say about their travel likes. Then decide which tour (1, 2, 3, or 4) is best for them. Write the number of the tour in the blank.

1. __3__ "I just love French food. I want to learn to cook it."

2. _____ "I need exercise. I'd like some warm weather too."

3. _____ "I like adventure. I don't want anything that's easy. I'm very healthy."

4. _____ "I enjoy different cultures. I don't like to see a lot of other tourists. I'm interested in Asian cultures."

5. _____ "I like adventure. I have only three days for my vacation."

6. _____ "I love food. I love all kinds of food. And I love Europe."

7. _____ "I like to swim and ride my bike. I love to go camping."

2 Here is a map of the Boston subway system. There are four lines: the Red Line, the Green Line, the Blue Line, and the Orange Line.

Here are some places to visit in Boston and the subway stops near them. Use the map to answer the following questions.

1. What line is the airport stop on?

   It's on the Blue Line.

2. What line is the Science Park stop on?

3. What line is the Symphony stop on?

4. What line is the Kenmore stop on?

_____

5. Is South Station on the Green Line?

_____

6. Is the Harvard stop on the Red Line?

_____

PART 4

Writing

Using Verb Tenses and Adjectives

Read the letter and look at the photo. Find examples of pine trees, rocks, and islands in the picture. Then answer the questions. Share your answers with a partner.

1. What activities does the writer talk about?
2. What can the writer see around him?

Dear Bill,
I'm here in Brunswick, Maine, a small town on the coast. My log cabin is old and weathered. Huge waves roll and crash against the jagged rocks. I can see beautiful green islands out in the bay. Tall and fresh-smelling pine trees are all around me.
   I'm reading a lot, swimming, and relaxing. I went fishing yesterday and caught a dogfish (that's a small shark). See you soon.

Jim

Adjectives make descriptions "come alive" (become interesting). The secret to good writing is to use only important, interesting adjectives that make a strong picture in the reader's mind. For example, compare the following two descriptions:

My log cabin is old *and* weathered.

Tall and *fresh-smelling* pine trees are all around me.

Notice that the adjectives help the reader form a picture in his or her mind.

Sometimes no adjectives are better than boring adjectives.

Along the shore there were big rocks and green pine trees.

Notice that *big* and *green* do not add very much to the writer's picture of the rocks and pine trees because we already know that rocks are usually big and pine trees are green.

Practicing the Writing Process

1   **Exploring Ideas: Free Writing.**   Write for ten minutes. Imagine you are on a great vacation. Write down a list of things you will do. Imagine what you can see. Do you see trees? The ocean? Are you in a city? Do you see many people? Write at least seven things you can see. Don't worry about spelling or grammar.

2   **Writing the First Draft.**   Write a postcard or a short letter like the one from Jim. Tell where you are, what you are doing, and what you can see and hear and smell at your imaginary vacation place.

Dear _____,

_____

_____

_____

_____

_____

_____

_____

_____

_____

_____

                              _____

3   **Editing.**   Notice the verb tenses in the short letter from Jim—the present tense
("I'm here"), the present continuous tense for the actions that are continuing ("I'm
reading a lot"), and the simple past tense for the actions that happened and are finished ("I went fishing"). Review your letter and check all the tenses. Did you use
them correctly?

   Use the following checklist to correct any mistakes.

Editing Checklist

Does every subject have a verb?

Do your sentences begin with capital letters?

Do other words in the writing need capital letters?

Do your sentences end with periods or other final punctuation?

---

4   **Writing the Second Draft.**   Now write the second draft of your letter. Be sure to
include interesting adjectives. When you're finished, give your letter to your teacher.

Writing a Journal

Here is a journal entry written by Jim, the same person who wrote the short letter.
Notice that this is a narrative—it uses only the past tense.

June 25, 2001

   Today I had a great day. I sat on the porch of the house. From there I
could see out across the bay. Along the shore there were rocks and pines
trees. The islands looked like round, green bumps where the sky met the bay.

   I sat in an old pine porch chair with my feet up on the porch railing. The
breeze from the ocean felt cool against my face. I read a little, then I looked
out on the water, then I read a little more. Everything made me feel alive and
happy—the sharp smell of the pines, the crisp feel of the ocean breeze, the
very blue sky and ocean. I wanted the morning to last forever.

Write a journal entry about one day on a vacation that you took. Use the simple past
tense. What details can you include to make a stronger picture in the reader's mind?

Video Activities: Cancun

Before You Watch.

1. The resort city of Cancun is in

   a. Spain.   b. Thailand.   3. Mexico.

2. What activity do people usually not do at a beach resort?

   a. visit museums   c. go scuba diving

   b. go swimming   d. go sailing

Watch.

1. Most activities in Cancun are on the

   a. water.   b. beach.   c. island.

2. Check the things that you can do in Cancun:

   _____ parasail   _____ go in a submarine

   _____ scuba dive   _____ swim with turtles

   _____ take a helicopter ride   _____ snorkel

   _____ ride in a glass-bottom boat _____ meet famous people

   _____ visit Isla Mujeres

Watch Again.   Complete the sentences with the numbers in the box.

10	20	25	2	30	2 to 3

1. Isla Mujeres is about _____ miles from Cancun. It takes about _____ minutes to get there by boat. The boat ride costs $ _____.

2. You can go parasailing in Cancun. It costs about $ _____ to parasail for _____ minutes.

3. Party boats are not expensive. For about $ _____ you can have lunch and go snorkeling.

After You Watch.   Imagine you are in Cancun. Write a postcard to a friend. Describe Cancun to your friend. Then tell your friend what you did yesterday, what you are doing now, and what you are going to do tomorrow.

Chapter 10

Our Planet

IN THIS CHAPTER

You'll read about one possible solution to an environmental problem. You'll also read the story of one international student who is helping our planet. And you'll write about a problem and a solution.

PART 1

The Greenhouse Effect and the Women of Guatemala

Before You Read

1 Look at the pictures that follow. Then answer the following questions with a partner or a group.

1. Why did someone cut down these trees? How will people use these trees?

2. What problem is the factory causing?

3. There are five kinds of energy here. Which kinds of energy do people use in your country?

a.

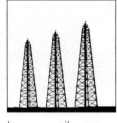    

b.   oil   coal   sun   wind   water

2 **Vocabulary Preview.**   Read the following sentences to help understand the meanings of the underlined words. Then answer the questions. Don't use a dictionary.

1. Factories send <u>gases</u> such as CO_2 into the atmosphere.

    What is one example of a gas? _____

2. Factories send gases such as CO_2 into the <u>atmosphere</u>, the air around the earth.

    What is the atmosphere? _____

3. Trees <u>absorbed</u>, or drank in, CO_2.

What does *absorb* mean? _____

4. We should learn to use different kinds of <u>energy</u>: the sun, wind, and heat from volcanoes.

What are three examples of energy? _____

5. There is too much CO_2, and there aren't enough trees, so the world is getting warmer. In other words, we have a <u>greenhouse effect</u>.

What happens in a greenhouse effect? _____

Read

3   Read the article. Try to understand the meanings of new words without using a dictionary.

The Greenhouse Effect and the Women of Guatemala

[A]   Most people know something about the greenhouse effect. Factories send gases such as carbon dioxide, or CO_2, into the atmosphere, the air around the earth. In the past, this wasn't a problem because trees absorbed, or drank in, CO_2. But now people are cutting down billions of trees in many countries. At the same time, factories are sending more CO_2 into the atmosphere. It's difficult to believe, but factories put billions of tons of CO_2 into the atmosphere every year! One ton is 2000 pounds, so this is a lot of pollution. There is too much CO_2, and there aren't enough trees, so the world is getting warmer. In other words, we have a greenhouse effect. This is terrible for the environment.

[B]   What can we do about this? First, we can stop using so much coal and oil. We can learn to use different kinds of energy: the sun, wind, and heat from volcanoes and from inside the earth. Second, instead of cutting down trees, we should plant more trees. One tree can absorb ten pounds of carbon dioxide every year.

[C]   In the past, the mountains of Guatemala, in Central America, were green and thick with beautiful trees. But people cut down trees for houses. Also, many women cook over wood fires. They walk hours every day to look for firewood. There are fewer and fewer trees, and this is bad for the land. Rain washes good soil down the mountains.

[D]   Far away from Guatemala, in the state of Connecticut, there is a new factory. The factory uses coal. It will send 400,000 tons of CO_2 into the atmosphere every year. Many people are angry about this. But the factory owners are doing some-thing about it. They are giving 2 million dollars to the women of Guatemala. The Guatemalans will plant trees in their country. These trees in Central America will absorb the carbon dioxide from the factory in Connecticut.

[E]   Why Guatemala? Why don't people in Connecticut plant the trees in Con-necticut? The answer is easy. Trees grow much faster in Central America than in the northern part of the United States.

[F]   The trees are good for the earth's atmosphere. They're good for Guatemala too. In small towns and villages in Guatemala, most women are poor and have hard lives. Trees help them in three ways. First, the Connecticut factory pays them to plant the trees. Their pay is corn, not money. The corn is food for their children. Second, these women know a lot about their environment. They know where to plant, when to plant, and what kinds of trees to plant. For example, they plant many fruit trees. The fruit gives them vitamins in their families' diets. Other trees are good for firewood. In a few years, the women won't spend so much time walking for wood. Third, all these trees are good for the soil. Now rain can't wash the soil down the mountains so easily.

[G]   This plan isn't enough to stop the greenhouse effect. But it's a beginning. The women of Guatemala are helping themselves and helping their environment. As one woman says, "We're planting for our families, for our children."

After You Read

4 **Finding the Main Ideas.**   Circle the number of the main idea of the article.

1. The greenhouse effect is a problem in the world today.

2. We should stop using coal and oil and use other kinds of energy.

3. A new U.S. factory is making people angry because it uses coal.

4. Women in Guatemala are planting trees, and these trees are helping the women's families and the environment.

Which information from the article explains the main idea? Write the information in the boxes.

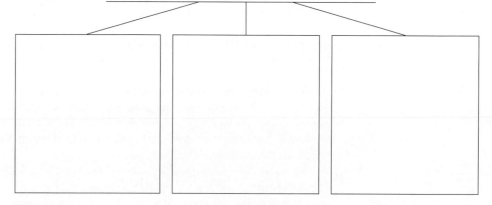

Main Idea: Trees are good for people and the environment.

5   Read the following sentences. If the information is not in the article, cross out the sentence. If the information is given, which sentence from the article has the information? Write the sentence.

1.   Trees absorb carbon dioxide.

    One tree can absorb ten pounds of carbon dioxide every year. _____

    _____

2.   All trees are beautiful.

    _____

    _____

3.   Trees give people fruit.

    _____

    _____

4.   Trees need too much water.

    _____

    _____

5.   Trees give people wood for fires.

    _____

    _____

6.   Trees are good for the land.

    _____

    _____

Cross-Cultural Note

In your country, do people talk about the greenhouse effect? Are there groups (such as TreePeople discussed in Chapter 7) who plant trees in your country?

6   **Making Good Guesses.**   Which fact can you guess from the article? Circle the letter of the answer.

a.   Trees are important.

b.   Connecticut is in the western part of the United States.

c.   The women of Guatemala are rich now.

Discussing the Reading

7   Discuss your answers to the following questions with a group.

1.   Are there many trees in your neighborhood? In your country?

2.   What kinds of energy are important in the United States? What kinds of energy are important in your country? What environmental problems do you have in your country?

PART 2   The Ocean in Trouble

Before You Read

1   Look at the pictures. Then answer the following questions with a partner.

1.   Is fishing important in your country?
2.   Do you know of any problems for the fishing industry?

2 **Vocabulary Preview.**   When we add *over* to a word, it can give it the meaning of "too much" or "too many" or "more than is good or healthy." Follow the example and fill the blanks with the missing words.

Example

If you overeat, you eat __too__ __much__ and you may get sick.

1. If you overwork, you work _____ _____ and you may get overtired.

2. If you oversleep, you sleep _____ _____ and you may be late for work.

3. If a place is overcrowded, there are _____ _____ people and you may feel uncomfortable.

4. If people overfish an area, they take _____ _____ fish out of the ocean and they may destroy the ocean environment.

3 Circle the word in each group that does not belong.

1. cure   smoking   disease   doctor

2. home improvement   baseball   garage   house

3. actors   scientists   marriage   entomologists

4. counselor   psychiatrist   artist   psychologist

5. sad   uneasy   happy   anxious

6. bugs   diet   insects   bees

7. fruit   corn   food   money

8. suddenly   then   nice   next

9. Titian   Rubens   Freud   Picasso

10. cola   toaster   coffee   caffeine

4   Read the information in italics and the sentences. Then answer the questions.

Remember that the information in parentheses after a word will often tell you the meaning of that word.

1. Trawlers (large fishing boats) are using new technology.

    What are trawlers? _____

Don't forget to look after dashes for the meaning.

2. Governments should create no-fishing zones—areas where no one can fish.

    What is a "no-fishing zone"? _____

The context of the sentences around the word can also give the meaning.

3. The story about pollution received a lot of publicity. There was more media attention than ever before.

    What is publicity? _____

4. Trawlers (large fishing boats) are using special nets fitted with wheels and rollers. They drag these across the bottom of the deep oceans, and they pick up anything of any size at all.

    What do trawlers do with the special nets? _____

    _____

    What do the nets do as a result? _____

    _____

Read

5   Read the following article. Try to understand the meanings of new words without using a dictionary.

The Ocean in Trouble

[A]   Many environmental groups are warning that the oceans of the world are in great danger. The two main dangers for the oceans are pollution and overfishing. Pollution receives more publicity, but overfishing may be the most destructive of the two in the next few years.

[B]   By the early 1990s, 13 of the world's 17 main fishing areas were already destroyed or badly damaged by overfishing. For example, the Grand Banks off the coast of Newfoundland in the north Atlantic was officially closed to fishing a few years ago. The fish have almost completely disappeared.

[C]   Fishermen are finding fewer and fewer fish everywhere. Unfortunately, this does not mean that fishermen are stopping fishing. Instead, many are using new technology to fish new waters as deep as a mile. Trawlers (large fishing boats) are using special nets fitted with wheels and rollers. They drag these across the bottom of the deep oceans, and they pick up anything of any size at all. These nets take species like squid, skate, red crabs, slackjaw eels, spiny dogfish, and orange roughy. A few years ago people didn't want to eat these species. Now you can find them in fish stores, in "fish sandwiches" at McDonald's, or in fake "crab meat" for seafood salads.

[D]   One example is the orange roughy. This fish appeared in fish stores only about ten years ago, but already the species is almost extinct. The orange roughy lives very deep in the ocean—up to a mile—in the cold waters off New Zealand. Scientists now know that fish in deep cold water grow and reproduce very slowly. For example, the orange roughy lives to be 150 years old. It doesn't start to reproduce until it is 30 years old. Although the fish is nearly extinct, people still sell it in seafood stores and in restaurants. And, of course, it may be in that fish sandwich you are eating at McDonald's.

[E]   Many scientists believe that present fishing methods will destroy all the large fishing areas of the world. What can be done to stop this?

[F]   Some scientists think that governments should stop the fishing industry from using some kinds of technology. But this will be difficult. Many of the big fishing companies have a lot of money, and they use that money to influence politicians all around the world.

[G]   Other scientists believe that governments should create no-fishing zones— areas where no one can fish. Governments can patrol and police these areas. During the U.N. International Year of the Ocean, more than 1600 leading marine scientists and conservation biologists from 65 countries urged the world to create 80 times the no-fishing areas that exist now. Their goal is to protect 20 percent of the world's oceans by 2020. This is happening in some places—for example, the fishing industry in Britain is beginning to accept no-fishing zones because the amount of fish the industry catches is getting smaller and smaller.

[H]   The fishing industry often argues that the scientific evidence is not complete—that we just don't know what is going on in the oceans. Now, scientists and environmentalists have to prove that the fishing industry is doing damage before the government will pass laws protecting the ocean. This takes time and sometimes it is difficult to prove something like this. *Science* magazine says we should have the opposite rule—big fishing companies should have to prove that they are not destroying the oceans before we allow them to fish. In other words, the companies should have the burden of proof.

[I]   Environmentalists say that average people need to get together and put pressure on their governments to do something; the large fishing companies who own the big trawlers are not going to stop fishing by themselves. If we don't, they say, there will be nothing left in the oceans but water.

6 **Finding the Main Ideas.**   Circle the number that states the main purpose of the article.

1. to give the reader information about why the fishing industry is important

2. to help the reader understand how the fishing industry works and also understand about deep water fish like the orange roughy

3. to tell the reader about the problems caused by overfishing and about no-fishing zones as a possible solution

7 The article "The Ocean in Trouble" is a kind of writing that presents a problem and a possible solution. We can call it "problem/solution writing." Read the following outline of this kind of writing. It is an outline of the article. Then do the exercise.

Introduction to the problem

1. details and facts about the problem

2. reminder of the problem and asking for a solution

3. possible solutions

4. arguments about the cause of the problem

Conclusion—a reminder of the need for a solution

Now assign each paragraph letter (A–I) to the outline. Some blanks will have more than one letter.

_____A_____ Introduction to the problem

_____ 1. details and facts about the problem

_____ 2. reminder of the problem and asking for a solution

_____ 3. possible solutions

_____ 4. arguments about the cause of the problem

_____ Conclusion—a reminder of the need for a solution

Discussing the Reading

8 Answer the following questions. Then discuss your answers in small groups.

1. Do you like to fish?

2. Is fishing important in your country?

3. What do you think about the article? What solution to the problem of overfishing do you support?

PART 3   # Information about Garbage and Trash

1   The graph below tells how many pounds of garbage a person makes on each day in 11 cities. Look at the graph and answer the questions.

Pounds of Garbage Produced per Person per Day

Los Angeles	6.4
Philadelphia	5.8
Chicago	5.0
New York	4.0
Tokyo	3.0
Paris	2.4
Toronto	2.4
Hamburg	1.9
Rome	1.5
Calcutta	1.12
Kano, Nigeria	1.0

1. Who makes more garbage each day—a person in Tokyo, Japan, or a person in New York City?

   A person in New York City makes more garbage each day.

2. Who makes more garbage each day—a person in Toronto, Canada, or a person in Los Angeles?

3. Who makes more garbage each day—a person in Calcutta, India, or a person in Paris, France?

Circle the correct answer to complete the sentences.

1. Five people in Kano, Nigeria, make the same amount of garbage each day as
    _____.

    a. two people in Rome

    b. one person in Chicago

    c. two people in Toronto

2. Five people in Calcutta, India, make about the same amount of garbage as
    _____.

    a. three people in Los Angeles

    b. two people in Chicago

    c. one person in Philadelphia

2 Read about Mark and Tony. Then answer the questions.

Mark recycles his metal cans. He takes them to a recycling center so they can
be used again. He doesn't throw any out. He recycles his paper products. He
puts his yard waste in a pile and puts it on his garden later. Here is a list of
what he put in the trash today. (Note: 16 oz. = 1 pound.)

metal cans	3 oz.
food waste	7 oz.
yard waste	0 oz.
paper products	2 oz.
glass bottles, jars, etc.	4 oz.

1. How many pounds of garbage did Mark throw out?

    _____

2. That is the average for what city?

    _____

3. How about you? What did you throw out today? Make a list.

    _____

    _____

    _____

    _____

    _____

    _____

Tony throws out a lot of things. Today he threw out the following things. Use the following list and the graph on page 161 to answer the questions about Tony.

bottles	14 oz.
soda cans and tin cans	8 oz.
1 newspaper, some letters, a magazine	30 oz.
extra food	12 oz.
yard waste	16 oz.

1. How many pounds of garbage did Tony throw out? (Hint: Add the total ounces, then divide by 16.)

    _____

2. Tony's garbage was exactly average for his city. Where does Tony live?

    _____

3   In the United States, many things are in our garbage. Look at the following pie chart and answer the questions.

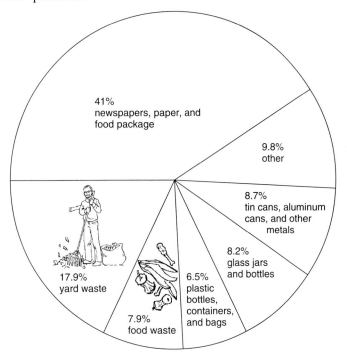

41%
newspapers, paper, and food package

9.8%
other

8.7%
tin cans, aluminum cans, and other metals

8.2%
glass jars and bottles

6.5%
plastic bottles, containers, and bags

7.9%
food waste

17.9%
yard waste

1. What is a larger percentage of our trash, newspapers or plastic bottles?
    Newspapers are a larger percentage of our garbage.

2. What is a larger percentage of our trash, yard waste or tin cans?

    _____

3. What is a larger percentage of our trash, glass or plastic bottles?

_____

4. What percent of our trash are metal cans and other metals?

_____

5. What percent of our trash are grass clippings and other yard wastes?

_____

6. What percent of our trash is food waste?

_____

PART 4   Writing

Analyzing a Composition

Read the student's problem/solution composition.

Paragraph 1: Introduction to the problem

One important problem in Los Angeles is the traffic. It has serious consequences, not only for the environment, but for people's well-being.

Paragraph 2: Details and facts about the problem

People own more than 5 million cars in the L.A. area, and it often seems as if all of them are always on the road. Someone estimated that people in Los Angeles spend 1.2 billion hours in their cars. Every morning and evening, movement on the freeways nearly stops. Even at strange hours like 10 o'clock at night, the traffic may suddenly stop.

Paragraph 3: One possible solution

Los Angeles just completed a subway, but this is not going to be a solution to the problem. People don't use it. They like their cars better. They want to be in control and drive exactly where they want. What can be done to change people's minds?

Paragraph 4: The writer's solution

In Singapore, drivers must pay extra money for using the freeways during the most popular hours. A computer system automatically charges cars. Los Angeles should build a system like this. The money that is charged can be used to build other kinds of transportation like more subways and improved buses.

Paragraph 5: Conclusion

The traffic problem in Los Angeles is becoming worse every day. We need a solution right now.

Can you think of a good title for this composition? Compare your answer with a partner's.

Practicing the Writing Process

1   Exploring Ideas: Free Writing.   You are going to write a problem/solution composition. Review the composition about Los Angeles traffic. It uses the same outline as the article "The Ocean in Trouble." Write down facts and details about the problem. Then write possible solutions. Don't worry about grammar, spelling, or punctuation.

2   Writing the First Draft.   Now write your first draft. Begin by completing the following topic sentence. Use the words in parentheses as a guide.

One important problem in my _____ (place) _____ is

_____ (the problem) _____.

To help you organize your paragraphs, go back to the outline of "The Ocean in Trouble" on page 160 or look carefully at how the composition about Los Angeles traffic is organized. If you are writing this composition as a homework assignment, you should include facts and statistics about the problem. You can do this by using library references or the Internet. If you are writing in class, you probably will not be able to include facts and statistics, but you still can add examples and other information that you know.

3   Editing.   Here's a list of things to check in your composition.

Editing Checklist

Is there an introduction, development paragraphs, and a conclusion?

Is there a title?

Are the verb forms correct?

Do your sentences begin with capital letters?

Do other words in the writing need capital letters?

Do your sentences end with periods or other final punctuation?

Is your spelling correct?

---

4   Writing the Second Draft.   Write your second draft and give it to your teacher.

Video Activities: Recycling

Before You Watch.

1. What are these things usually made of? Write P for paper, A for aluminum, G for glass, or PL for plastic. More than one answer may be correct.

   _____ soda cans

   _____ shampoo bottles

   _____ cereal box

   _____ magazines

   _____ wine bottles

   _____ light bulb

2. What is the best way to get rid of trash?

   a. Burn it.   b. Bury it.   c. Recycle it.

Watch.

1. Edco is a company that _____.

   a. buys trash   b. makes trash   c. recycles trash

2. Check the kinds of trash that you see.

   _____ milk bottles

   _____ bones

   _____ clothes

   _____ dishes

   _____ newspapers

   _____ cans

Watch Again.

1. Number the steps in the recycling process.

   _____ Workers sort the trash into piles.

   _____ Edco sends recycled material to customers.

   _____ Workers collect the trash.

   _____ Large trucks dump the trash at Edco.

After You Watch.   Write a paragraph about trash in your community. Think about these things. What do people do with their trash? Do they burn it? Do they bury it? Do they dump it on the land? What are some solutions to the problem of trash?

Photo Credits